Get Ready for Physics

Physics

EDWARD ADELSON

The Ohio State University

Addison-Wesley

Boston Columbus Indianapolis New York San Francisco Upper Saddle River
Amsterdam Cape Town Dubai London Madrid Milan Munich Paris Montréal Toronto
Delhi Mexico City São Paulo Sydney Hong Kong Seoul Singapore Taipei Tokyo

DEDICATION

To Julie, whose faith in my abilities has never wavered.

Publisher: Jim Smith
Director of Development: Michael Gillespie
Development Editor: Mary Katherine Hager
Editorial Manager: Laura Kenney
Senior Project Editor: Katie Conley
Senior Marketing Manager: Kerry Chapman
Managing Editor: Corinne Benson
Production Project Manager: Beth Collins
Production Management, Art Creation, and Composition: GEX Publishing Services
Cartoonist: Kevin Opstedal
Copyeditor: GEX Publishing Services
Interior and Cover Designer: Seventeenth Street Studios
Photo Editor: Donna Kalal
Manufacturing Buyer: Jeff Sargent

Photo Credits: Page 9: Ryan McVay/Photodisc/Getty Images, Page 37: Tom Stewart/Corbis, Page 181: From Sears, Zemansky, and Young, College Physics, 7th ed., ©1991 by Addison-Wesley Publishing Company. Reprinted by permission of Addison-Wesley, Inc., San Francisco, California.

Addison-Wesley
is an imprint of

www.pearsonhighered.com

ISBN 13: 978-0-321-55625-7
ISBN 10: 0-321-55625-9

2 3 4 5 6 7 8 9 10—CRS—14 13 12 11 10

Contents

Welcome to the most fundamental and most fascinating of the sciences. Although most students take physics because it is a required course, those who go beyond trying to memorize the minimum in order to pass can begin to acquire a deep understanding of how we live in a universe ordered by natural law.

Many students struggle with physics, but we know that the reason is often not a deficiency in ability, but the result of trying to treat it as a series of facts rather than as the history of our struggle to wrestle the appropriate concepts out of the natural world. Research on how physics is learned has shown that we must use observations and experimental results to develop conceptual understanding before any name we apply to that situation has meaning or any formula we learn can be employed correctly.

Because lectures cost a school less than recitations, it is all too easy to become convinced that you need to memorize what your teacher lectures on. But your real learning will come when you work on developing your own understanding, whether it is while reading the textbook or solving homework problems. When a homework problem gives you serious difficulty, remember that you must look at what is going on, the conceptual framework of the problem.

This book is designed to lead you through a sufficient number of basic concepts to enable you to learn a strategy that will help you work through the rest of a first-year course on your own. Whether you go through as much of it as you can before your class starts or use it along with your class material, its purpose is to help you get a strong start in physics and to develop the conceptual understanding that will serve you for the rest of your life.

This book starts with basic study skills in **Chapter 1**. As with any course, you will get out of physics what you put into it. Even those who have already been introduced to physics concepts will need to put in significant time and effort to succeed, but those who bring a wholly "common sense" approach to the subject will need to put in a great deal of extra effort because changing beliefs in any area is as difficult a task as growing up and changing childish ways for mature ones. This chapter helps you focus and manage your time so you can first find time to study, then use your study time effectively. You will learn how to use your preferred learning style to your advantage, but do remember that we all can learn in many different ways. You'll assess your habits as a student and learn specific tips and strategies to help you study better. This will help you take notes, read textbooks, and use homework to obtain real understanding. In turn, that will help you to succeed on tests.

Chapter 2 covers the math skills that are used most often in beginning physics courses. The most important skill is the ability to work quickly and correctly with algebra, particularly proportional reasoning. You will use right angle trigonometry often, but logs and exponentials to a lesser extent. An important tool in obtaining conceptual understanding is the ability to go between equations and their graphs. This chapter also covers scientific notation and significant figures.

In **Chapter 3** we first introduce kinematics, the description of motion; then the two basic approaches—solving by force laws or by conservation theorems, such as conservation of momentum and energy—are introduced.

If you concentrate particularly on any one chapter, this is the one you should master. The concepts introduced here are used in every other area of physics. Even when new concepts such as temperature or electric charge are introduced, we have to deal with the energy of the bodies and the forces between them.

Chapter 4 introduces you briefly to static electricity; magnetism; thermodynamics; oscillators; optics; and atomic and nuclear physics. The major part of your physics textbook cannot be covered in one chapter of a short book, but the introductory concepts will be familiar to you when you start to study these subjects.

In **Chapter 5**, we isolate the methods and strategies that will provide the greatest help when doing homework and taking tests. If you do not have time to go through this whole book thoroughly, concentrate on Chapters 2, 3, and 5.

Some special features in each chapter include the following:

- *Your Starting Point* tests your grasp of chapter content before you start. Answers are provided for all of these except in Chapter 1, where the answers are personal.

- *Quick Check* asks you to recall what you just read or worked on, to keep your eyes

from scanning the page in memorization mode without engaging your brain in conceptual understanding.

- *Time to Try* is a simple problem or quick assessment in which you actively participate in finding a solution.

- *Keys* highlight basic laws and major conclusions for reinforcement and easy review.

- *What Did You Learn?* This section provides a list of key topics and definitions. Use this list to test your understanding of these topics and definitions. In particular, if you cannot explain how to make a measurement to find a value for any physical quantity, such as velocity, it is a signal that you need to go back and put in more time on that topic.

- *Web Resources* are not listed specifically because there are so many good ones out there. At the end of each chapter you will find suggestions for how to locate additional help on the web.

This book tries to present topics in a logical order but in an informal style. Think of it as a treasure hunt where the gems are the concepts that illuminate our understanding of the world. It's time to get started. Get comfortable and dig in to *Get Ready for Physics!*

Acknowledgments

My interest in helping students started long ago when Randy Knight, now author of Pearson's book *Physics for Scientists and Engineers* was vice chair of the physics department at The Ohio State University. The day after I proposed a preparatory course to him because many students were less prepared as a result of initiatives to increase the number of students going to college, he informed me that we would have such a course, that I would teach it, and that the paperwork was due in 24 hours. This resulted in my writing two books for that course. The second, *All in Proportion*, has been in use for the last seven years.

Knowing of that book, Adam Black, who was the Pearson publisher for physics at the time, proposed that I contribute a volume to the *Get Ready* series. To him goes the credit for the initiation of the writing of this book. After Adam's promotion, Jim Smith, publisher for physics; Michael Gillespie, director of development; and Mary Katherine Hager, developmental editor, took over. I am grateful to them not only for all the help they provided, but also for their patience while I dealt with other pressing problems. I am grateful to Dyan Menezes, editorial assistant, for her help while the chapters were being written and then to Katie Conley, senior project editor, for her assiduity in making sure they were prepared for publication. Finally, many thanks to Marisa Taylor, senior project manager at GEX Publishing Services, for turning the manuscript into the final print version of the book.

I also wish to thank Evan Sugarbaker, vice chair for administration of the physics department at The Ohio State University, for his support while *All in Proportion* was being prepared, and then during the difficult time while I was writing this book. Most of all, I wish to thank E. Leonard Jossem, now deceased, for getting me interested in the results of physics education research and in training graduate teaching assistants. I thank Michele Kaufman Rallis, the other course manager, for being there to back me up.

Chapter 1 is a revised version of Chapter 1 in Lori K. Garrett's *Get Ready for A&P*, modified for physics students and their differing needs. Chapter 2, initially based on Chapter 2 in *Get Ready for A&P*, has been revised and greatly expanded because of the much greater need of physics students for many more mathematical topics, and for coverage of the common ones in greater depth. I am grateful to her for the permission to use this material, but I particularly thank her for the hard work that went into Chapter 1. A small amount of material has been taken from my book, *All in Proportion*. The modeling of Faraday's law from artificial data was originally employed in ISLE material by Alan Van Heuvelen and Eugenia Etkina.

Finally, I would like to thank those students who care enough about themselves and their futures to embark on their college educations with the extra lifeboat that this book is intended to provide. May they conquer the waves of difficulty they will encounter by putting in the extra effort needed to row to safety.

—Edward Adelson

1 | Study Skills: Know Yourself

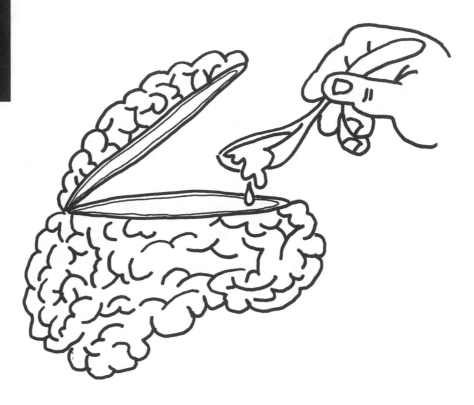

When you complete this chapter, you should be able to:

- Understand your preferred learning style and the study strategies that emphasize it.

- Have skills that will help you get the greatest benefit from lectures, recitations, labs, and readings.

- Have a written schedule that includes adequate study time.

- Know how to prepare well for an exam.

- Understand that you are ultimately accountable for your own success or failure.

Most physics courses meet four or five times a week for a standard 48- or 50-minute period. At most schools, physics courses also include a 2- or 3-hour lab. How would you handle such a course?

Your Starting Point

Answer the following questions to assess your study habits.

1. How often would you study for this course, as just described? _____

2. How many hours would you put in each time you studied? _____

3. Would you review your class notes daily? _____

4. Would you wait until exam time to put in most of your study time? _____

5. Where do you study (home, dorm room, library, somewhere else)? _____

6. Do you have distractions where you study, such as iPods, TV, or noisy roommates? _____

7. Are you able to plan a study-time schedule and stick to it? _____

8. Do you receive good support from family and friends? _____

9. Will you find enough serious-minded friends to form a successful study group? _____

10. When you are studying, do you stop frequently to ask yourself if you understand what you are reading, or whether you understand the process when solving a problem? _____

11. Do you check your work to see if it seems reasonable? _____

Welcome to the exciting and sometimes challenging world of physics. Physics teaches us how the world works: not just mechanical toys or gravity at the Earth's surface, but the rules that run the entire universe. As the first science to find mathematical correspondences to real-world actions, physics is the prototype for other sciences and engineering. Even gaming and movie animation computer experts study physics to make their characters' actions seem real.

Many of these physics rules had to be teased out by years of work—2,000 years in the study of the interaction between forces and motion. Those efforts were necessary because our common sense notions handle immediate perceptions without looking at what is behind them. This book will help you start to look "beyond the phenomena," of physics, review necessary math, and prepare yourself for effective study.

Why Should I Study Physics?

For many of you the answer to the question above will be, "Because it is required for my major," or "Engineering uses physics as a flunk-out course." But that ignores the benefits you might gain if you understand why physics matters. With that understanding you should not only end up better prepared to take a physics course, but you should find it easier to study the course material.

 PICTURE THIS

Suppose that until recently a grandparent of yours has been very healthy, but a serious medical problem has arisen. You are not likely to be able to help your grandparent with a health issue, so he or she seeks medical help for an analysis of the problem and, we hope, for a cure.

1. What knowledge must the doctor have to be able to accomplish that goal?

_____

_____

_____

2. Why does the doctor, or any other practitioner in the health field, need to understand physics?

_____

_____

3. In what ways are professionals in science and engineering similar to people in the health field?

_____

_____

4. Why do these science and engineering professionals also need to understand physics?

_____

_____

Physicians must understand everything about physics, from how to apply traction, to how to measure and interpret pressure of fluids in the body, to how to determine proper doses of radiation. Every interaction in nature demonstrates an action of physical law, though we may use other approaches such as chemistry and biology for the more complex interactions.

Most students taking physics will be working either in the health field or in engineering. Only a smaller number will be working in the nonapplied sciences. Much of engineering consists of application of physical laws to creating new, or improving old, machines and devices. Now consider your own future.

1. What career are you preparing for?

_____

2. Why will you need to know physics for that career?

_____

To Thine Own Self Be True: **Learning Styles**

What is the best way to learn physics? Many research papers have been published that describe experiments on learning. These investigations look at different aspects of the learning process. One of the ways to approach the question of appropriate learning styles considers which senses a learner relies on the most: sight, sound, or touch.

- Visual learners learn best by *seeing.*

  - Visual-linguistic learners like to learn through reading and writing.

  - Visual-spatial learners prefer viewing charts, demonstrations, videos, etc.

- Auditory learners learn best by *hearing.*

  - Auditory learners often like to repeat material aloud, and can be helped by using a tape or digital recorder.

- Tactile (kinesthetic) learners learn best by *doing.*

  - Tactile learners often benefit most from movement (kinesthetic) and touch (tactile) methods, such as using highlighters and taking part in activities.

TIME TO TRY

Let's find your preferred learning style with a self-testing approach. Note that all such tests oversimplify findings and that everyone uses all learning styles. However, each individual possesses a preferred way of learning.

Use Table 1.1. Read the activity in the first column, and then read each of the three questions in the column to the right. Circle the response that seems to correspond to the way you approach this activity. Then add the number of responses circled in each column. The column with the largest number of responses indicates your dominant approach to learning. The column with the next largest number indicates your secondary learning style.

TABLE 1.1   **Assessing your learning style.**

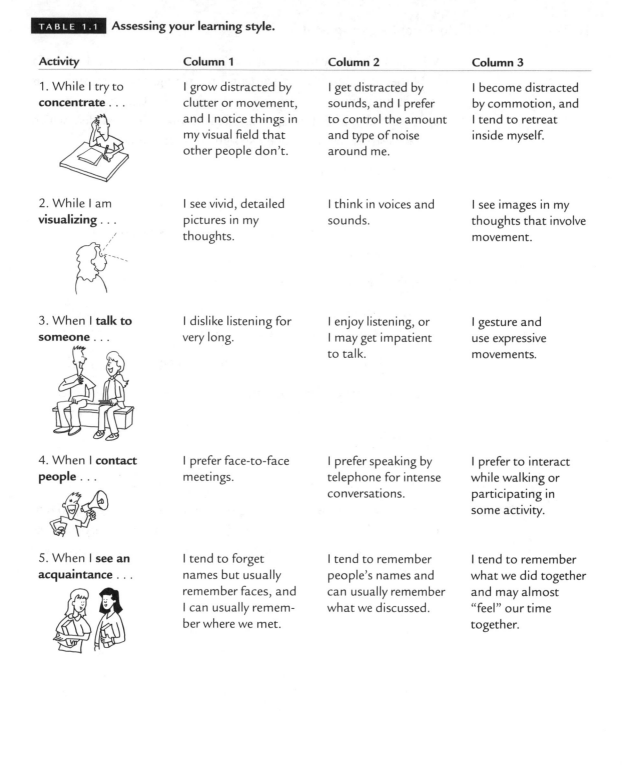

Activity	Column 1	Column 2	Column 3
1. While I try to **concentrate** . . .	I grow distracted by clutter or movement, and I notice things in my visual field that other people don't.	I get distracted by sounds, and I prefer to control the amount and type of noise around me.	I become distracted by commotion, and I tend to retreat inside myself.
2. While I am **visualizing** . . .	I see vivid, detailed pictures in my thoughts.	I think in voices and sounds.	I see images in my thoughts that involve movement.
3. When I **talk to someone** . . .	I dislike listening for very long.	I enjoy listening, or I may get impatient to talk.	I gesture and use expressive movements.
4. When I **contact people** . . .	I prefer face-to-face meetings.	I prefer speaking by telephone for intense conversations.	I prefer to interact while walking or participating in some activity.
5. When I **see an acquaintance** . . .	I tend to forget names but usually remember faces, and I can usually remember where we met.	I tend to remember people's names and can usually remember what we discussed.	I tend to remember what we did together and may almost "feel" our time together.

TABLE 1.1   **Assessing your learning style, continued.**

Activity	Column 1	Column 2	Column 3
6. When I am **relaxing** . . .	I prefer to watch TV, see a play, or go to a movie.	I prefer to listen to the radio, play music, read, or talk with a friend.	I prefer to play sports, make crafts, or build something with my hands.
7. While I am **reading** . . .	I like descriptive scenes and may pause to imagine the action.	I enjoy the dialogue most and can "hear" the characters talking.	I prefer action stories, but I rarely read for pleasure.
8. When I am **spelling** . . .	I try to see the word in my mind or imagine what it would look like on paper.	I sound out the word, sometimes aloud, and tend to recall rules about letter order.	I get a feel for the word by writing it out or pretending to type it.
9. When I **do something new** . . .	I seek out demonstrations, pictures or diagrams.	I like verbal and written instructions, and talking it over with someone else.	I prefer to jump right in to try it, and I will keep trying and try different ways.
10. When I **assemble something** . . .	I look at the picture first and then, maybe, read the directions.	I like to read the directions, or I talk aloud as I work.	I usually ignore the directions and figure it out as I go along.

▶

TABLE 1.1 **Assessing your learning style, continued.**

Activity	Column 1	Column 2	Column 3
11. When I am **interpreting someone's mood** . . .	I mostly look at his or her facial expressions.	I listen to the tone of the voice.	I watch body language.
12. When I **teach others how to do something** . . .	I prefer to show them how to do it.	I prefer to tell them or write out how to do it.	I demonstrate how it is done and ask them to try.
TOTAL:	**Visual:** _____	**Auditory:** _____	**Tactile/Kinesthetic:** _____

[Source: Courtesy of Marcia L. Conner, www.agelesslearner.com]

Summary:

My primary learning style is _____.

My secondary learning style is _____.

Now you can plan your studying to emphasize activities that employ your preferred learning style. Look closely at your scores. If two of the scores are close, you already use both of these styles when studying. If your high score is much higher than your other scores, you have a strong learning preference and should emphasize that style. Most people use a combination of learning styles.

Note that information entering through different senses reaches different parts of your brain. The more of your brain that is engaged in processing information, the more effective your learning will be, so you should try strategies for all three styles of learning while emphasizing your preferred style over the others. You'll discover which approaches work best for you. Some strategies that you might try for each style are listed in Table 1.2.

TABLE 1.2   **The three learning styles and helpful techniques to use in your studies.**

 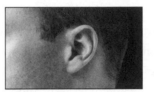 

	Visual	**Auditory**	**Kinesthetic /Tactile**
Techniques to use	❏ Sit close to the teacher and the blackboard.	❏ Listen carefully to your teacher's voice.	❏ Highlight important information while reading.
	❏ Take detailed notes; be sure you can understand them later.	❏ Read the textbook and your notes out loud.	❏ Write your own notes during class and while reading the textbook.
	❏ Draw sketches and diagrams.	❏ Tape or digitally record lectures and listen to them later.	❏ After class, recopy your notes neatly or type them on the computer.
	❏ Use graphs.	❏ Spend more time listening in class than taking notes.	❏ Sketch and diagram each physical situation as you read.
	❏ Use flow charts and flash cards to review definitions and basic equations.	❏ Work in a study group.	❏ Place objects on your desk to simulate those described in your reading or in a problem you are solving.
	❏ Focus on figures, tables, and their captions.	❏ Discuss the material with others.	❏ Try to create and conduct your own experiments, as long as they can be carried out safely.
	❏ Visualize symbols as the distances, forces, etc., that they represent.	❏ Go to your teachers' office hours for more discussion.	❏ Hold your book while reading.
			❏ Walk or stand while reading.
			❏ Use flash cards to review definitions and basic equations.

Caveat: Good physics teachers try to provide alternate explanations in addition to those in the textbook, as well as different examples. Students must combine taking notes with listening when such explanations and examples are given, no matter what their preferred learning styles might be.

VISUAL LEARNERS

If you are a visual learner, you rely heavily on visual cues. You notice your teacher's expressions, gestures, body language, and particular quirks. Because seeing these cues is especially helpful to you, you should sit at the front of the classroom, close to the teacher. You tend to think in pictures and learn well from visual aids such as diagrams, illustrations, tables, videos, and handouts. Here are some strategies for you:

- In class, take detailed notes and make sketches.

- When studying on your own, draw pictures that relate to the information and convert the pictures to diagrams, graphs, and bar charts. Make flow charts and concept maps; use flash cards; and focus on figures, illustrations, graphs, and diagrams in your textbook, and read the accompanying captions.

- Convert all problems into pictorial sketches. Then convert them into motion diagrams, free-body diagrams, work-energy bar charts, and any other such diagrams introduced in class, lab, or the textbook. Look these diagrams up on the Web if they are not in your textbook or presented in class.

- Use mental visualizations of the topic you are studying and imagine yourself acting out processes. Use books or other objects on your desk to represent bodies in physics examples and problems. Push or pull on them, or lift or drop them to feel and see the examples. Try imagining that you are the moving body, you are driving the car, or you are the body the forces are acting on.

    Note: If you are in the sub-group of visual learners with photographic memories, you will be able to see pages of the text or blackboard mentally but must beware of using that as a substitute for understanding.

AUDITORY LEARNERS

If you are an auditory learner, you learn well from traditional lectures and discussion. You listen carefully to your teacher's pitch, tone, speed, and mannerisms. Material that you struggle with while reading becomes clearer when you hear it. Here are some strategies for you:

- Read the textbook and your notes out loud.

- Tape or digitally record the lectures so you can listen to them later. Recording lectures also allows you to listen during class instead of focusing on writing, which is less beneficial for you.

- Work in a study group, and discuss material with your teacher, lab group, and friends. Participate actively in group work in recitation if your school offers this opportunity. If you attend a large lecture, make a particular effort to avoid passive listening by jotting down questions that occur to you during class and discussing those with classmates and your instructor. Then seize any opportunity to ask those questions in recitation or laboratory classes.

- Avoid listening to iPods or other MP3 players, radio, and TV while studying. Find a place for studying that lacks distracting sounds.

TACTILE LEARNERS

If you are a tactile learner, you learn best by actively participating and doing hands-on activities. You may become bored easily in class from sitting still too long and start fidgeting or doodling. You need to do something physical while studying and learning. Here are some strategies for you:

- Try using a marker to highlight important information while you are reading.

- Write out your own notes in class and while reading the textbook. After class, recopy your notes or type them into your computer. However, be careful not to miss your professor's explanations of difficult concepts by trying too hard to take notes at those times.

- Draw sketches of physical situations and turn them into diagrams or graphs as you read.

- Create and conduct your own experiments, particularly when studying the mechanics portion of the textbook.

- Hold your book and walk while reading.

- Make and use your own flash cards for important concepts, laws, and equations.

- Keep your hands and your mind busy together.

WHY SHOULD I CARE?

Understanding your own learning style allows you to develop more effective and efficient study techniques that take advantage of your sensory preferences. When you emphasize your preferred learning style, the material will be easier to understand and will stay with you longer.

✔ QUICK CHECK

Making sketches and turning them into diagrams and graphs would be most helpful to which two learning styles?

_____ and _____

How could they be used by a learner of the third style?

Answer: They would benefit visual and tactile learners. An auditory learner could describe them out loud and record the descriptions for later repetition. He or she could also discuss them with friends in a study group to be sure they were understood correctly.

Getting Ready

Don't wait until the first lecture to start thinking about classes. The key to a good start is to be organized and ready when you enter the classroom. This takes advance planning, but the time invested will save a greater amount of time during the semester.

PUT IT IN WRITING

What are your goals this semester/quarter? When you begin a project without setting goals in advance, you may just drift along. If you set a goal, you enter with a purpose and a direction. Take time *now* to think about your goals for the semester. They should be both specific and attainable. Be realistic.

It may not be realistic to aim for the highest total score in the class, but a grade of A might be attainable. Be honest about the number of hours of work per week this might require, usually a minimum of at least two hours of study for each hour spent in class.

Once you've decided on your goals—and don't forget to include leisure time, sports, and dating, as well as classes—write them down both to give them more importance and to list them in order of priority. If you find that you've given more emphasis to play than to study, you may want to reconsider your priorities. But once you've completed this task, be firmly committed to the goals and priorities you have set. (As you go through college, you will find that you accept more responsibility, so your goals will change in a positive way.)

Now write these goals on an index card and place the card in a prominent location in your study area so you'll see them every day. You are working on establishing habits, but don't fret if you miss keeping to your goals because of forgetfulness or sickness. Just get back on track as quickly as possible.

TIME TO TRY

Now let's set goals specifically for physics:

Set three main goals for yourself in this class, and write them in the spaces that follow. Explain why achieving each goal is important to you.

Goal 1. _____

It's important to me because _____.

Goal 2. _____

It's important to me because _____.

Goal 3. _____

It's important to me because _____.

PULL IT ALL TOGETHER: ORGANIZATION FOR CLASS

It's hard to believe, but students show up for tests without anything to write with, with a malfunctioning calculator, or with no calculator at all. Don't let that happen to you. The better organized you are, the more efficient you will be. List and categorize items you might need for coursework as those you take to class every day, those used at home when studying, and those that may be useful but are not essential. Start with the checklist in Table 1.3 and modify it to fit your particular classes. You probably already have many of these items at home. Many are available at discount stores. The rest can be bought at your college-area bookstores.

Keep all the items you need for class in one place: a book bag, backpack, or briefcase. If it contains the essentials, you are always ready to head out to class without a room-destroying search.

What should you pack?

1. A pocket-sized day planner with plenty of room for writing. You can keep this with you all the time. Alternatively, a personal organizer portfolio or an electronic organizer will do the job. Select what you like best. Write all important dates you already know in it: when classes begin, holidays, the last day to withdraw from a class without a mark on your record, the last day to withdraw at all, and when final exams begin. Enter all class times and room locations, your work schedule, and any other known time commitments such as team or band practice times. This will also let you review how your time has been spent. Then you can make modifications to use your time more efficiently.

2. A to-do list, either one that is part of your day planner, or one separate from it. This item will be a lifesaver. Write all assignments and due dates on this list. There should be just one list for all classes and nonschool activities, because your time must be divided between them. By writing dates and tasks down, you can review the entire list and the deadlines for each item. That compiles priorities so you can complete assignments in the order in which they are due.

TABLE 1.3 Organizer's checklist.	
Item	✎✗
To take to class each day:	
Book bag/backpack/rolling carrier	
Textbooks/lab manuals	
Pocket-sized day planner	
To-do list	
Separate notebooks for each course	
Copy of class schedule with buildings and room numbers	
Several blue or black ink pens	
Several #2 pencils	
Small pencil sharpener	
2–3 colored highlighter pens	
Small stapler	
Grade record sheet for each course	
Calculator	
At home:	
Master calendar	
Separate file or folder for each course	
Loose notebook paper	
Index cards	
Computer paper	
More writing utensils (pens and pencils, colored markers/pencils)	
Stapler	
Calculator	
Scissors	
Paper clips	
Optional:	
Personal organizer	
Small tape recorder to record lectures/readings	
Recording tapes	
Extra batteries for tape recorder, calculator	
Dictionary	

3. A record of all grades you receive (see Figure 1.1). List each graded item, when it was submitted, and when it was returned, if it was hand-graded. You will need to do this for quizzes and exams, and possibly for homework and labs. List how many points you received, for this may be the only feedback you get for computer-graded homework, the maximum possible scores, and any additional notes. Most teachers explain how your grades will be determined during the first class; you can use this information to keep track as you go along. Your record also provides a back-up in case of any later confusion about your work and your grades entered in your teacher's or teaching assistant's grade book. Always keep any graded materials, exams, quizzes, lab note-books, and homework until the end of the semester or quarter, so you will have them in case grading questions arise. Never write on your work after it is returned; instead, write correct answers for what you missed in your notebook. That way you can avoid being accused of altering an answer when you bring the material in as proof of a grade.

Check with your instructor to see if you should bring your textbook to class. In physics, you may not need it for noninteractive lectures but will be more likely to need it in recitations. Check also whether your text is needed in lab. If your course uses a lab manual, always take it to lab. This is especially vital if your work is done in the lab manual.

And always carry the basics. You will need a notebook for note tak-ing in lecture. You will also most likely need a notebook for recitations,

Item	Date Turned In	Date Returned	My Score	Maximum	Notes
Lab 1	9/6	9/13	97	100	Worked with Emily and Shawn
HW 1	9/9	9/9	16	20	Get help with prob. 37
Quiz 1	9/9	9/14	13	15	Restudy def'ns; memorize

FIGURE 1.1   An example of grade record keeping.

although some schools may provide special group workbooks like the University of Washington "Tutorials," or the equivalent in special recitation handouts. In lab, you may work directly in the lab manual, or may have to write in a special lab notebook that you hand in and receive back at the next lab. Alternately, you may have to record data in your notebook and hand in the report later in the week or during the next lab. Make sure you know *exactly* what your class's procedures are and what materials are required.

Make sure you have all other necessary materials with you: pens, pencils, erasers, paper, highlighters, colored pencils—used by some teachers to indicate different types of vectors—staples, a small stapler, index cards, and paper clips. Replenish your supply before you run out completely.

Set up your dorm or home study space as much like a home office as possible. Have all essential supplies, pens, pencils, papers, etc., on hand. Be sure to display a master calendar, either a desktop or wall version prominently. You could use a calendar feature on your computer, but the more visible the calendar, the more often you will look at it. Think BIG, because anything you add to your day planner or to-do list should be added to the master calendar. Enter all time commitments, your class schedule, exams, study sessions, and even your personal appointments and vacations. If you schedule your life this way when in school, the practice will stick with you far beyond that.

If you are reading this after starting classes, you can still get organized. It's never too late to "get it together."

✔ **QUICK CHECK**

To be successful in class, your effort should be to start before class begins. What are some tasks you should do before the first day of class?

_____

_____

_____

Set and write down your goals, be sure you have the items you will need for class and at home, pack your carrier, start your day planner and master calendar, and organize your study space.

I Hate to **Lecture** on This, but Can You Hear Me Now?

Welcome to class! Imagine it is the first day. You walk into class.

Where do you sit? _____

Why do you sit there? _____

The best seat in a classroom is front and center. Obviously not everyone can sit there, but you should arrive early enough to sit within the first few rows and as near to the middle as possible. You want an unobstructed view of the instructor and of all the demonstrations because experiment is the basis of all physical science. People sitting on the sides or in the back of the room often don't want to be called on, or want to avoid engagement with the class. Don't let that be you. To succeed, you need to focus all your attention on your instructor, minimize distractions, and participate actively. Instructors tend to teach to the middle of the room (Figure 1.2). If your instructor is right-handed and uses equipment, such as an overhead projector that is positioned to his or her right, the instructor's focus shifts to the right. You want to see your instructor, and you want your instructor to see that you are present, actively listening, and engaged. This is even more important in large classes where instructors can't get to know all students; you may need to ask for a reference later on, and you can get a better one if the instructor knows who you are.

Some instructors provide lecture notes, even podcasts, so you can sit back and really think about what is being said during class. Notes or not, you need to get all the information you can from each lecture. Remember your learning style and use techniques that enhance it. Consider taping or digitally recording the lectures. Then you miss nothing and can listen repeatedly, rewinding as necessary, and only need to copy the equations on the board during class. A good technique is to write out your notes while listening to the recording; then listen again and make necessary corrections. This reinforces the material strongly.

Always try to preview the material that will be covered before going to class. This can require as little effort as skimming the assigned sections of the textbook. The material will then sound familiar and will be easier to comprehend when your instructor covers it in class. The

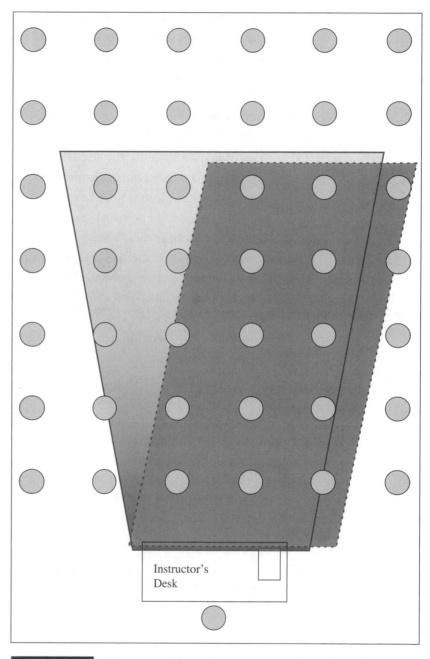

Instructor's
Desk

FIGURE 1.2   Main areas of focus for an instructor. The large shaded area shows where the instructor looks most often. The smaller shaded area shows how that focal area shifts to the right as the instructor uses equipment positioned to the right.

important thing in physics is to understand why new concepts are introduced and what they correspond to in the world. Only when you understand these relationships will you be able to use the math that corresponds to these entities correctly. You can find equations in the book; understanding what the symbols mean, how they are defined, and how they are related is what you need to get from classes.

Don't hesitate to raise your hand to ask a question or get clarification. Many students are shy and reluctant to speak in class—they fear being embarrassed in public. Be the confident, assertive person and ask the question. You'll be doing the rest of the class a favor. But wait until after class to discuss personal issues with the instructor. That is better done alone, outside the classroom.

Note your instructor's gestures, facial expressions, and voice tone for clues about what your instructor finds most important. That material is likely to show up on a quiz or test. Write down any material that is particularly emphasized and mark it in your notes. Listen carefully for assignments and write them immediately on your to-do list. If the syllabus, class policies, and assignments are posted on a website, check it frequently, not just for assignments but for any information about approaching exams and any changes in exam rooms and/or dates. If anything about an assignment is not clear, such as which problems are assigned, when the work is due, or what topics are being covered, seek immediate clarification.

✔ QUICK CHECK

Why is it best to sit front and center in class?

_____

_____

Answer: You will be more engaged in the class, have the best view and fewer distractions, and be within your instructor's focal area.

Passing Notes

How can you take notes that are good enough to help you succeed in the course? Of the many strategies and models for note taking, find what works for you and then use it consistently. We'll review one easy-to-use system (see Figure 1.3).

```
                 09/15/10
RECALL:
Note          I.    Note taking tips
taking
                    A. Use outline format

                    B. Be concise; uz shrthnd

                    C. Get main ideas first, then eqs.

Reviewing     II.   Reviewing Notes

                    A. Review quality of notes after class

                       1. Fill in gaps

                          a) ask classmates for clarification

                          b) use textbook if necessary

                       2. Clean up, clarify confusing notes, etc.

                       3. Make sure signs and factors
                          in eqs. are correct

                    B. Review content of notes as soon
                       after class as possible

                       1. Helps move material to your
                          long-term memory

                       2. Replay lecture in your mind

Three        III.   Learning styles
learning
styles               A. Visual—reread and add diagrams/graphs

                    B. Tactile—rewrite or type

                    C. Auditory—read out loud or tape/digitally record
```

FIGURE 1.3   Sample of lecture notes using the outline style and leaving room in the left margin.

Start with a full-sized (8.5" × 11") notebook—a composition book or a loose-leaf binder—that you will use just for this class. Write only on the first side of each page and leave about a 2" margin on the left. The margin will be used for marking key definitions and equations. At the beginning of class, date the top of the page so you know when the material was covered. (This is very important for those who prefer loose-leaf paper.)

During lecture, use an outline format so you can get the maximum information down in the minimum number of words. Use each main concept as a major heading; then indent the information on that topic. At the end of the topic draw a horizontal line and leave a couple of lines blank. Don't even try to get down every word, just the main ideas. If possible, put them in your own words. Use a brief summary or a one- or two-word reminder for examples gone over quickly. Demonstrations involving prediction, experiment, and discussion should get their own major or minor subheading. Use abbreviations when possible and develop your own shorthand. U cn oftn drp mst vwls in a wrd n stll b abl to rd it ltr. Write legibly! Underline new definitions, equations important enough to have received a derivation, and, in particular, any discussion of how common-sense ideas conflict with the definitions of terms in physics when those terms, such as force, position, work, etc., are also used in everyday speech with different meanings. Use a star or an arrow to indicate anything that is emphasized. Remember, this is an outline. The instructor won't wait for you to catch up, so you must get down quickly what will help you learn the material from your notes *and* the book.

As soon as possible after class, read your notes and improve them as necessary. Add anything that's missing, particularly algebraic steps that lead from one equation to another. For instance, you may be told that by solving $v = v_0 + at$ for t and substituting it in $x = x_0 + v_0 t + \frac{1}{2} at^2$, you can obtain $v^2 - v_0^2 = 2a(x - x_0)$. Do the algebra and check it out for yourself: That will make it easier to remember signs and factors of 2 in all three equations.

Make your notes clearer and cleaner. Put the concepts in your own words. Next, use the left margin to summarize each section—the main concepts, subtopics, and key terms. That column will be your "recall" column. Once you are sure all of the key ideas are in the left column, you can cover the right side of the page—the meat of your notes—and test yourself on the main points listed on the left. It makes an easy way to review, though it cannot substitute for the learning that occurs when you also solve extra, unassigned problems before a test.

But you are not finished. If you are a tactile learner, rewrite your notes in another notebook or type them into your computer. Visual learners might type and reorganize the notes. (For physics you will need a word program with an equation editor.) Auditory learners can read the notes out loud or record them.

You can turn equations and definitions into flash cards by writing the term defined or a description of the equation on one side of an index card and the definition or equation on the other side. You can add sketches. A good way to practice how to go from describing a physical situation to identifying a solution would be to put a sketch of a situation on one side of an index card and an equivalent diagram or graph on the other side. Whatever you do, review your notes as much as you can during the next 24 hours after class, while the lecture is still fresh in your mind.

TIME TO TRY

Look at the sample notes in Figure 1.3. Now practice by watching a 1-hour educational show on public broadcasting or a nature channel. While viewing, capture the main points, action, and demonstrations in words and/or sketches. You can't get everything down, so paraphrase—put concepts in your own words so the meaning comes across. When you're finished, assess how you did:

Can you tell who was talking?

Do your notes make sense?

Did you capture the main ideas?

Did you keep up or fall behind?

Do you have breaks in your notes to separate the main topics and actions from one another?

Do you have headings for the main topics and actions?

What can you do better while taking notes in class?

✔ **QUICK CHECK**

What should you do with your notes after class?

Answer: Review them within 24 hours; fill in anything missing; clean them up; put them into your own words; add key concepts, terms, and equations to the recall column; add drawings; make flash cards; and record, rewrite, or type your notes.

How to Get the Most out of Recitations and Labs

Most physics courses have recitations. With very few exceptions, all algebra and trig-based or calculus-based courses have labs. A number of schools have introduced "studio" courses in which lecture is reduced to a minimum and recitation and lab are combined into group work, both problem solving and experiments. We'll take up traditional recitations first.

TRADITIONAL RECITATIONS

The traditional recitation may take either of two forms or a combination of them. In one variation, students are called on, either as volunteers or at random, to put solutions to homework problems on the board. In the other, the teacher or teaching assistant (TA) solves problems for students, usually asking which problems students want to see solved. There is only one way to benefit from this type of recitation: Do the homework *before* class and make a list of problems you could not solve and of any points that were not clear to you. You can then ask the teacher for help with those. Other students also benefit when you do this, but not as much as you, because their minds are not prepared for understanding.

✔ **QUICK CHECK**

What are some of the advantages of attending traditional recitations?

Answer: You may get a chance to solve a homework problem with help from the instructor or may have the instructor solve the problem for you.

NONTRADITIONAL RECITATIONS

In nontraditional recitations, students work in groups on problems too difficult for any one student to solve alone. The auditory students can contribute by expressing the problem in words students can understand. The tactile students can imagine performing the experiments and gain a feel for the results. The visual students can help by making sketches, diagrams, and graphs. The differing talents of students within a group combine to solve problems in difficult contexts. Once the technique has been learned, students gain deeper insight, and, amazingly, make faster progress than students in traditional recitations. In a nontraditional recitation, you may also be given incorrect solutions and be asked to find the errors, or be given a solution and be asked to find a problem that has that solution. Because employers value the ability to work well in groups, this experience makes students who take such courses more valuable employees.

Group work must be managed to be effective. One student should act as a recorder for the group; another should act as manager. One should be a skeptic who makes sure that the group does not go with the first, and possibly incorrect, suggestion. A fourth student should act as an energizer and encourage the group to keep on working when the going gets hard. Groups should have three or four students for maximum effectiveness. Ideally, group members should be selected by the teacher on the basis of diagnostic tests. If you are allowed to choose your own partners, look for serious collaborators, not for high school friends who may end up wasting class time on off-topic discussions.

The teacher or teachers—some such recitations have two or three teachers—will circulate or be available for questions.

✔ **QUICK CHECK**

What are some of the advantages of attending nontraditional recitations?

Answer: You will get practice at working in groups, a skill valued by employers. You will also achieve deeper insight into the topic and make more progress than students in traditional recitations.

LABS

Labs also are offered in traditional and nontraditional forms. In a traditional lab, you take data and show that the data fit a known law. Conversely, you may try to find an equation that fits the data and then compare it to a known law. A statistical analysis may be required. This helps you understand the physical basis of laws and under what experimental conditions the laws are valid. Students work in groups in lab because there is not enough equipment for each student to have a setup, and because more than one pair of hands is often needed in running an experiment.

Nontraditional labs are more complex in nature. You may be given equipment and asked to design an experiment that can be performed with that equipment. You will be given sufficient guidelines so that you don't flounder around for the whole period, but you must prepare for the lab in order to possess the theoretical skills needed for planning the experiment and the tactile skills required for carrying it out. Some sort of analysis of how good or accurate the results are will be required. The auditory member(s) of the group will have to help with discussion at all points in the lab. You won't be asked to reinvent the wheel, but these labs will bring you as close as possible to discovery as one can get in a 2- or 3-hour class.

Don't disregard the lab component; it's the hands-on part of the course. Many people learn better by making predictions, seeing the demonstrations when doing the work themselves, and reconciling differences between results and predictions. Remember that part of your grade comes from the lab. Always do any assigned prelabs before the lab and bring necessary materials.

You will work with a partner or group. Be prepared so that you can contribute equally and not be disdained as a "free rider." Pay attention to instructions and safety precautions.

Don't take shortcuts or leave a bit early. Lab is where you explore the material covered in lecture and recitation and get a deeper conceptual understanding of it. Collaboration and discussion are every bit as valuable here as in group work in a recitation. It is unfortunate that traditional lectures are not often in synch with the lab, but the lab is part of the same course and may very well be where you have an "aha" moment, especially if you are a tactile person.

✔ **QUICK CHECK**

What are some of the advantages gained from attending lab sessions?

_____

Answer: You see the relationship between data and laws, you are able to explore with equipment, you receive hands-on learning, and your participation involves collaboration and discussion with a group. Lab sessions are also where you may have an "aha" moment.

The more time you spend in lab, the better you will see the relationship between the mathematical model and the physical system. ■

STUDIO COURSES

At some schools, lecture, lab, and recitation are combined into one. Students work in groups, with computers and equipment available at all times. Teachers manage discussions but lecture as little as possible. These "studio" courses start out slowly, but by giving students a firm grasp of the basics they are soon ahead of the standard lecture courses both in topics and in difficulty of material covered. This takes a bit of getting used to, especially by those who like to work independently, but the students in studio courses are grateful when they have to use the physics learned in such a course in engineering courses or in medical school.

REALITY CHECK

Answer True or False to each of the following statements:

1. I study the day before a test but rarely on a daily basis.   T F

2. I mostly review my notes and don't need the textbook.   T F

3. I am too busy to study each day.   T F

4. When I finally get around to it, I study pretty hard for a long time.   T F

5. I get by fine with cramming.   T F

JUST FOR FUN

Let's see how good at studying you *really* are! Take a few moments to learn these terms. We will come back to this exercise a bit later.

1. **Sputi missilis.** An enemy mugwumper with an arc parametrization.

2. **Leidenjerk grabacider.** An emasculated monkeyjunker, high on the lab ceiling, that has an instaurated adumbration of eternal infelicity.

3. **Expurgated wavicle.** A timewise-flummoxed invisible quantum guillotine that destroys cats-o-nine-lives in alternate universes.

Stay tuned!

You made it through today's class and are ready to head home. School is done for the day, right? Not if you plan to be successful. The real work begins after class because most of your learning occurs outside the classroom, on your own. This is often the hardest part, for many reasons. Sometimes we schedule too many activities and set time aside for them, but cram studying into spare moments. Too often studying becomes what you do when you "get around to it," and it gets dropped from the to-do list.

Too many students only study when they have to—before a quiz or exam. A successful student studies every day. The goal is to learn the material as you go rather than frantically try to memorize a large amount at the last minute. Here is something you need to know and really take to heart:

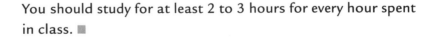

You should study for at least 2 to 3 hours for every hour spent in class. ▪

If you have three lectures on Monday, for example, you should plan to spend from 6 to 9 hours studying that same day. YIKES!

Here are some suggestions for making the most of study time.

SCHEDULE YOUR STUDY TIME

Writing assignments on your to-do list helps keep you from forgetting them, but that does not cover work that must be done daily for each course. You must take charge of your time and studying. In addition to specific assignments, each day you ought to do the following:

- Go over that day's notes.

- Reread the corresponding sections in the textbook.

- Check your understanding.

- Start on the homework problems that are labeled as corresponding to the textbook sections currently assigned.

- Reread your notes and the corresponding sections in the textbook to clarify difficulties with the homework.

- Prepare for the next day by reading the sections assigned for those classes.

This process takes time. You must build study time into your schedule; otherwise, you will not get around to it, or you will put it off until you are too tired to study effectively. First, write your study time into your day planner and master calendar. Next, regard that time as inviolable; never borrow from it to do something else. Third, plan break time during study sessions; spend too long on a task and your brain will become weary and start to wander. Plan a 10 to 15 minute break for every hour of study time. Also, stretch briefly every 10 to 15 minutes. Fourth, alternate subjects. Rather than studying two hours on physics and then two on math, spend one hour on physics, one on math, another on physics, and then another on math.

DIVIDE IT UP

We tend to put off jobs that seem too large but manage better with many small tasks. Break your workload into small chunks. Write them down, partly in order not to forget any, but mostly to gain a feeling of accomplishment when each is completed and crossed off your to-do list.

When a task is completed, it's time to take a *small* break to keep your mind fresh. Don't try to read a whole chapter or cover a few weeks of notes in one sitting. The brain has seven to nine random-access registers, and really dislikes your constantly cramming them full. Divide a large amount of material into subcategories, then study one until you really understand it before moving on to the next.

There is one exception: When your time is limited, it's better to skim a chapter on the next day's class material rather than not to look at it at all.

STUDY ACTIVELY

Merely reading your notes or the book is not learning. Copying problem solutions from a model in the book, a friend, or the Web also contributes little to learning. (You may memorize the solution to that particular problem, but physics is about solving *new* problems.)

You must think about the material and become an active learner. Constantly ask yourself, "What is most important in this section?" Don't skip over derivations; fill in the missing steps so you understand when and how to use the results. Solve as many problems as you can. Use the easy exercises to make sure you understand what symbols and terms represent. Recognize that such exercises are trivial. Do as many problems as you have time for where you first have to analyze the physical situation and then deduce the relevant mathematical relations. You can check the answers for the odd-numbered problems in the back of your textbook.

As you study, take notes. Outline derivations and the results on index cards. Put the important equations on flash cards and test yourself to be sure you know what each symbol represents and to determine that factors of 2, minus signs, and exponents are correct. If you are not given an equation sheet on exams, this activity is vital. Underline new definitions and key concepts, especially concepts that conflict with common-sense ideas. Apply these ideas to familiar situations while being careful not to revert to preconceptions. (We'll look at examples in later chapters.)

Practice, such as that previously described, is the best preparation for quizzes and tests. Develop and answer questions as you read. Keep a list of points you did not understand, so that you can get help from your lecturer or recitation instructor. Try to anticipate all the ways your instructor might quiz you about that material. Recall which specific items your instructor stressed. Outline the material in each section and be sure to understand how different concepts are related. Check yourself as described in the previous paragraph. Read definitions out loud and make sure you are not confusing terms with different everyday meanings. (For instance, you can push on a wall with all your strength until you are exhausted, but because physics defines work as a product of force and displacement, no work is done on the wall if it doesn't move.)

MOVE PAST MEMORIZING

This is one of the hardest study traps to avoid. When you are studying it can seem as if there are too many chapters and too little time. A new movement in physics has been emphasizing fewer topics with deeper learning, but this philosophy has not yet reached the majority of schools. Most students, therefore, first attempt to get by with memorization. If you only read your notes and the book, and copy solutions to homework problems, this is the approach you are using.

At the beginning of this section, you were given three items to learn. Without turning back, write down the three names I asked you to learn a few pages back:

1. _____

2. _____

3. _____

Did you remember them? Now, also without turning back, can you write down each definition?

_____

_____

_____

(I am betting not.)

These three "things" are fictitious, though those who know Latin would have recognized "a missile of spit" as one of them. The point is that you may have memorized the names—it doesn't take much to memorize a little bit—but it takes a lot more to understand them, especially if the words are unfamiliar or are used in unfamiliar ways, as they often are in physics. If you find that you study hard but the wording of the quiz or test confuses you, you are probably relying on memorization and making use of unchallenged common-sense ideas. When a question is worded differently, or a problem is reversed, it varies from what you memorized, so you don't realize you know the answer. As Virgil's Aeneas declared about returning from the underworld, "This is the task, that is the hard work." Reading produces memorization—which is why I remember that Virgil passage—but active studying produces understanding.

USE CONCEPT MAPS

A useful technique for learning relationships is drawing a **concept map**. This is somewhat like brainstorming, and similar to what happens inside the brain when a concept registers through your eyes or ears. Here is the general process:

1. Start with a blank piece of (preferably) unlined paper.

2. Draw a circle near the center, and write the main concept you will explore inside it.

3. Around that circle, and allowing some space, draw more circles and list in each anything that pops into your mind as being related to your main concept. Do this quickly and don't think about the relationships yet. Just get your ideas down.

4. After you have added all your secondary concepts, look at them and think about how they are related, not just to the main concept, but to one another as well.

5. As relationships occur to you, draw arrows connecting related concepts and add a brief description of the relationship beside the line connecting each pair of concepts.

6. Examine the relationships and you will start to understand how they fit together. The better you understand and the harder you work at the material, the better your concept maps will be; they will then help you obtain further understanding.

TIME TO TRY

Constructing a concept map for physics is somewhat difficult to do when you haven't yet learned the concepts and their definitions as given in your physics course. You may have some questions. But construct a concept map around the main concept of *force* by adding arrows to show relationships between the following concepts:

- acceleration

- mass

- velocity

- work

- energy

- displacement

- friction

- kinetic energy

- thermal energy

First, draw a circle or node for each concept. Keep the main concept, if there is one, near the middle. Next, add arrows linking the different concepts to one another, and then add brief descriptions of how they are linked. How circles might be drawn for these concepts is shown in Figure 1.4.

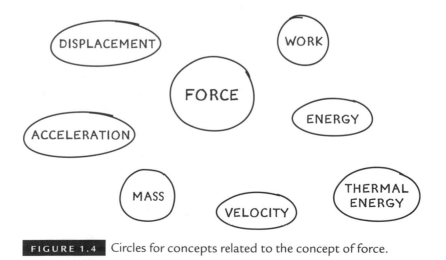

FIGURE 1.4 Circles for concepts related to the concept of force.

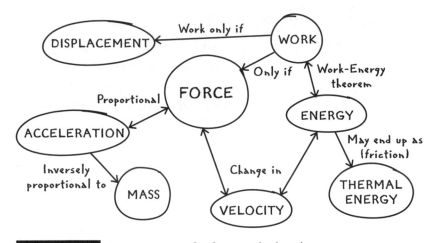

FIGURE 1.5   A concept map for force and related concepts.

If you have not already done so, draw in lines connecting these concepts. When you are finished, look at Figure 1.5.

In this example the arrows show that acceleration is proportional to force and depends on mass. The arrows connecting work to force and displacement show that a force may do work when the object undergoes a displacement; other arrows show that this results in a change of energy and velocity of the object. The concept map also indicates that some of this energy may end up as thermal rather than kinetic energy.

REVIEW

Okay, you've been at this study thing for a while, and you think you're starting to get the material. You followed all of the suggestions in this chapter; can you quit now? Almost, but once you think you have the material under control, review it one more time. Repetition is the key to your long-term memory—the more you go over the material, the longer it will stay with you—and long-term memory is the key to doing well on exams. A minimum of three passes is the least that is necessary, even for easy stuff: Read your notes, read the text, reread your notes—and that assumes you are understanding the material, including the assigned homework. Always slow down and go through it again if you are struggling with a certain section. Also remember that you learn physics by working at conceptual exercises and problems, not by memorizing the text.

Use *active learning* with each pass, and then finish with one more review. If you are alert enough to review right before going to bed, your brain often continues going over the material while you are asleep.

The website for your textbook also provides a good way to review. The URL is in your book. Most book websites offer a variety of activity options. When taking quizzes online, do so as you would in class. If you are not allowed to have an equation sheet in class, take an online quiz without your book and notes. If you do well online, you will have confidence in the classroom. Remember that material presented online is not as detailed and as much in depth as the material covered in class.

Once you have made the effort to review material effectively, practice habits that help you to retain the concepts and to get sufficient rest to permit clear thinking. One strategy is to avoid watching TV before bedtime. A recent study has shown that viewing more than 1 hour of TV at night interferes with sleep in adults.

NO CRAMMING ALLOWED

If you are busy, your dorm room or apartment may get cluttered up. If your parents call and say they are on the way, you might grab some clutter and cram it into a closet. After your guests leave, you open the closet to pull out a blanket. What happens?

Now imagine what you do to your brain when you cram for an exam. You are opening the closet door and cramming stuff in, then slamming the door. While taking the test, you open the door to pull out the answer you need, but anything might tumble out onto your paper. At best, cramming allows partial short-term memorization. At worst, it causes the information to get mixed up and you fail. Cramming is a desperate act of superficial studying guaranteed *not* to get you through physics. If you study on a daily basis instead of doing a panicky cram session before a test, you will be calmly reviewing what you already learned well and smiling at the crammers in the class.

NO VAMPIRES ALLOWED

Do you think you can pull an all-nighter and really do well?

What, in your opinion, are some of the reasons why this will not work?

If you normally live your life by day, you cannot suddenly override your natural biological clock and expect your brain to stay alert and focused when it knows it is supposed to be asleep. Caffeine may help keep your eyes open, but you'll only be a tad more alert and jittery while still yawning and mentally drifting from the task at hand. The only reason for staying up all night is that you have not studied adequately all along, so that staying up is your last option. It is not effective. You will not be mentally alert. You will not be able to focus or think through the material. Your eyes may skim the pages, but you'll struggle to comprehend the words. The next day you will find it difficult to solve equations, and you'll retain less than half of what you absorbed the night before.

An all-nighter is just a marathon cram session held at the worst possible time. It robs both your brain *and* your body of what they need: restoration before the next day. You may be able to stay up all night, but if you doze off you may oversleep and miss your exam. Or, if you do arrive (I hope you weren't driving with no sleep), you may get part way into the test only to have your brain bail on you. If you are prone to "test anxiety," your defenses will be down and you will quite likely freeze and fail. If only you had been studying all along....

For your brain to be kind to you, you have to be kind to its home. You must take care of yourself physically: eat wholesome food, get enough sleep, exercise regularly, and *relax*. ■

✔ **QUICK CHECK**

Why should you study every day if the test is not for two weeks?

Answer: Studying on a regular basis breaks the material into smaller, more manageable pieces that you can master. The material is fresh in your mind, and you will only need to review it before the test.

Strength in Numbers: **The Study Group**

One of the best ways to learn anything is to teach it to someone else, so form a study group or discuss the material with others around you (see Figure 1.6). This benefit is one reason why so many colleges and universities are introducing group work into recitations or changing traditional courses into studio physics courses where all work is done in groups. A few schools even organize class groups by dorm. This group approach is highly effective for most students.

As soon as possible, start asking your classmates if they would like to be in a study group—you *will* get people to join. You can test each other, discuss the material, help each other, and, quite importantly, support each other. If you study alone, you may not be aware of your weaknesses, particularly your preconceptions that impede the learning of physics. Your study partners can help identify your deficiencies while you help identify theirs; then you can all work together on overcoming them.

One way to work in a study group is to split up the material and assign different sections to different members, when possible. (This only works in physics for sections that are relatively independent of one

FIGURE 1.6 Study groups can be very helpful for staying motivated and focused on course material.

another.) The member responsible for a section masters that material and teaches it to the group. Each member must also study all of the material on his or her own; that ensures better effort from everyone, and allows other members to correct any errors in a presentation.

In schools where group work is organized formally, one student will be assigned the job of manager to keep the group on task. Another will be the recorder, who gets everything down on paper or on screen. The third will be the skeptic, the person who makes sure that the group doesn't just go with the first idea, but rather makes sure that the group gets on the right track. A fourth group member can be an energizer to keep the group working when the going gets rough. Three or four members form an ideal group. Two is too few; five or more is unwieldy, with members who are observers rather than participants.

Scheduling group sessions can be challenging. This is another reason for keeping a group to three or four members. Many students find that scheduling group sessions before or after class works best. You also need to establish ground rules, including agreeing to use the time for studying and not for gossip or socializing. (Here's where the group manager comes in.) And although it may be tempting to meet over pizza, you want to choose a quiet location where you can discuss the material freely with few distractions. In large schools, some classrooms might be free, particularly early or late in the day. In small schools you can probably get your instructor's permission to use an unoccupied classroom or lab.

SQR Huh? **How to Read a Physics Textbook**

The name may sound odd, but SQR3 is an effective method for studying a textbook. This method also works well when reviewing your notes. Science textbooks do not read like novels, so you must approach them differently. (The version of SQR3 presented here is modified to take into account the peculiarities of physics textbooks.) SQR3 stands for

- Survey

- Question

- Read

- **Recite**

- **Review**

During the **survey phase,** read the chapter title, the chapter introduction, any other items at the beginning of the chapter, and all of the headings. This gives you the road map of where you will be going. It corresponds to the instruction given to speakers: "First tell them what you are going to tell them." As you skim the chapter, also read all sentences that have words in bold or italic type for definitions of terms and symbols, and look at all equations that are boxed or have a colored background. You can skip over derivations at this point, but try to get an idea of what each section is explaining, and a sense of what is important. This is the minimum preparation for lectures on those sections. Also look at the chapter summary at the end of the chapter. If it consists principally of equations, that is a warning that you will need to go back and read carefully if the concepts behind the equations are to have any meaning.

During the **question phase,** which in physics should be combined with reading the sections, look at the heading of each section, and try to form as many questions as you can think of that may be covered in that section. Questions that should come to mind are the following:

1. What is the main point of this section?

2. What evidence has been given to support that point?

3. What examples and/or applications has the author provided?

4. Can you think of any other relevant examples?

5. How is this section related to the main topic of the chapter? How is it related to the rest of the book, to the physical world, and to me?

If you keep these questions in mind, you will automatically search for answers as you read.

Now **read** the chapter section by section. Read each section for details. Take your time. Question each sentence. Do the algebra to derive each equation from the preceding equation(s). At the same time, search for answers to your questions and fill in the missing steps in derivations, but avoid marking up the text until you are sure you understand what really is important.

The next phase is to **recite.** You are working on your ability to recall information. After reading each section, think about your questions and try to answer them from recall. Can you remember the main conceptual and mathematical results? Even if you don't remember equations expressing physical laws exactly, do you now have an idea of their general form?

At this point my recommendations diverge from the standard SQR3 method, the review step. Don't review endlessly: Start doing **homework** problems. Start with the easy ones. Make sketches, graphs, and diagrams as necessary. List all known and unknown quantities. Then attempt a mathematical representation of that information. Select the physical principle(s) that will give you the equation or equations that connect the known and unknown quantities. You will probably need to refer back to the examples in the textbook, particularly at the beginning. A basic mistake many students make is to try to do the homework, with reference to the examples, without first reading the book. That approach leads to memorization of a repertoire of examples without acquiring deep understanding. In a course where conceptual understanding is valued, that will be a disaster. Also, don't stick only to problems that require you just to substitute numbers in equations. Begin on the harder problems where you need to think more deeply about the principles and how to represent the physical situation in your own words, diagrams, and math.

At this point you will not only have gone through the chapter, but you will also have much of your homework done, especially the problems matched with particular sections in the text. Now you want to **review.** This helps reinforce your memory. Go back to each section heading and see if you can still answer all of your questions. Repeat the recite phase until you can do so, but not necessarily in one study session or on one day. Also remember that you may need help from your lecturer and recitation instructor in order to overcome preconceptions that clash with what you are reading. If you have worked hard and the material is still confusing, you may need this help. Also be sure you put some time in on physics—and on *each* subject—*every* day.

Now you may want to highlight or underline important points and equations, and add notes in the text and margin. But remember that most students highlight too much and limit this effort. Finally, be sure you can also answer the end-of-chapter questions in the book.

Another thing you can do to review is prepare a one-page outline summary of each section. These summaries are very useful when doing homework and in reviewing for tests when you don't have time to reread the whole chapter. And *now* you are ready to complete the homework assignment.

✔ **QUICK CHECK**

What is SQR3 and what do the letters mean?

_____

Question, Read, Recite, and Review.
Answer: It is a system of reading a textbook, and the letters mean Survey,

A Place to Call My Own: **The Study Environment**

Briefly describe the location where you plan to do most of your studying:

_____

_____

Now you know how to study effectively, but, like many people, you might overlook *where* to study. Your options may be limited, so you need to make the best of what you have. Ideally your study spot is somewhat isolated and free of distractions like TV, music (including iPods or other MP3 players), and people. At the least you should minimize distractions.

Do you study in front of a TV that is on? Even if you try hard to ignore it, you will be drawn to it, especially if the material you are studying is tough. Music can be tricky—songs that you know, especially energetic ones, may get you tapping and singing along with them while you think your mind is actively engaged in learning. However, soft or classical music can keep you calm and more focused, unless that is the music that draws your attention.

Think about the study site you listed earlier: What distractions might you face?

_____

_____

How can you minimize them? _____

If you cannot, seek another study spot.

For studying, you really need a space that is your own. A desk is a good place (unless it's where you spend hours playing computer games for fun). Ideally it will be a place where you do nothing but study, so you know exactly what your purpose is when you are seated there. If you are having trouble staying on task in your work spot, get up and walk away briefly. The mental and physical break may help you come back to work, and you won't begin associating the spot with struggling. Your study location should be quiet, have good lighting to avoid eye strain, and provide a comfortable chair, good ventilation and temperature, and a work surface on which you can spread out.

You will spend a lot of time studying here, so take time initially when setting up your study space. The area should be uncluttered and well-organized. It should also be inspiring and motivational. Perhaps you can frame a sign that says "I will be a ____*(your career)*____ by ____*(your goal date)*____." Try this same approach for the goals you set at the beginning of this chapter and display them boldly and prominently. Consider displaying a photo of your hero or heroine, or of someone in your family whom you want to make proud.

Parents: You might display a photo of your children with a caption saying something like "You are my reason," or "I will teach by example." Realize that you are their role model. Your children's attitudes toward education will be formed by what you do now. With these treasures surrounding you, you're a mere glance away from being reinvigorated if a study session starts to fizzle out.

WHY SHOULD I CARE?

Most of your learning is done outside of class. The more efficient your studying, the better you will learn. Your study area affects your attitude and concentration. The more seriously you take your study location, the more seriously you will study there.

If you live with family or a roommate, you absolutely must stress to them the importance of respecting your study time and study space. In this aspect of your life as a student, you must not be overly accommodating. Be sure your housemates know your career goals and why they are so important to you. Ask them to help by giving you the time and space you need to succeed. Ask them not to disturb you when you are in your space. If you have small children who want time with mommy or daddy while you are studying, after making sure that they have adequate supervision, try getting them to play or study on their own until "the clock hands are in these positions," then do something with them at that time. They will learn to anticipate your time together and to leave you alone if the reward is worthwhile.

If you have too many distractions at home, the solution is to study elsewhere. Whether on campus, in the local library, or at a friend's house, you need a distraction-free setting. Remove yourself instead of trying to cope with a poor study space. If you live in a dorm with one or more roommates, it becomes even more important to find distraction-free study places. You need to make clear to roommates that you will not put up with any behavior that endangers your grades and your goals. If roommate problems get bad enough, do not hesitate to insist on changing dorm rooms. Involve your parents if necessary. But, of course, if you expect cooperation from your roommates, you must also cooperate in helping them study.

✔ **QUICK CHECK**

What are some of the main considerations in selecting your study spot?

_____

_____

Answer: Few distractions, own space just for studying, comfortable, good lighting and ventilation, sufficient work space, and welcoming.

My, How **Time** Flies!

You know you need to study and that it takes a lot of time, but how will you fit it in? Let's discuss a few ways to budget time for studying. First, be consistent. Consider your schedule to see if you can study at the same time every day. Studying will become a habit more easily if you always do it at the same time. Some students adhere to one schedule on weekdays and to a different one on weekends. When scheduling study time, consider your other obligations, as well as how distracted you might be by other people's activities at your study times. Don't overlook free hours you might have between classes while on campus. Head to the library, a study room, or a quiet corner. This is the ideal time to prepare for the next class or to review what was just covered.

TIME TO TRY

This is a two-part exercise designed to help you find your available study time.

Part A: Each week has a total of 168 hours. How do you spend yours? Table 1.4 on page 45 allows you to approximate quickly how you spend time each week.

1. Complete the assessment in Table 1.4 to see how many hours are left each week for you to study.

2. Enter that number here: _____ hours

Part B: Next, turn your attention to Table 1.5 on page 46.

1. Enter your class schedule, work schedule, and any other activities in which you regularly participate.

2. Now look for times when you can schedule study sessions and write them in.

3. Are you able to schedule 2 to 3 hours of study time for each hour of class time? _____

It can be difficult, but it is essential to make the time. Writing it into your schedule makes it more likely to happen.

TABLE 1.4 **Assessing how your time is spent.** For each item in this inventory, really think before answering and be as honest as possible. Daily activities must be multiplied by 7 to get your weekly total. One item may be done any number of times per week, so you'll need to multiply that item by the number of times each week you do it. After you have responded to all the questions, you'll have an opportunity to see how many hours remain during the week for studying.

Where Does Your Time Go? Record the number of hours you spend.	How many hours per day?	How many days per week?	Total hours per week: (hours × days)
1. **Grooming,** including showering, shaving, dressing, applying make-up, etc.			
2. **Dining,** including preparing food, eating, and cleaning up.			
3. **Commuting** to and from class and work, from door to door.			
4. **Working** at your place of employment.			
5. **Attending class.**			
6. **Doing chores** at home, including housework, mowing, laundry, etc.			
7. **Caring** for family, a loved one, or a pet.			
8. **Participating in extracurricular activities** such as clubs, church, volunteering.			
9. **Doing errands.**			
10. Enjoying **solo recreation,** including TV, reading, games, working out, etc.			
11. **Socializing,** including parties, phone calls, hanging out, dating, etc.			
12. **Sleeping,** including naps.			
Now add all the numbers in the column to the right to get the total time you spend on all these activities.			
		Hours/week	168
		Total hours spent on other activities –	
		Left for Studying **=**	

Don't overbook. Be sure to build in break time during and between your study sessions, especially the longer ones. Allow for flexibility. Realize that the unexpected occurs, so be sure you have some extra time available. Plan for and schedule recreation too. You cannot and should not study all the time, but these other activities do take time and need to be in your schedule as well, so that you do not double-book yourself.

TABLE 1.5 **My study schedule.**

Time	Monday	Tuesday	Wednesday	Thursday	Friday	Saturday	Sunday
6:00 AM							
7:00 AM							
8:00 AM							
9:00 AM							
10:00 AM							
11:00 AM							
Noon							
1:00 PM							
2:00 PM							
3:00 PM							
4:00 PM							
5:00 PM							
6:00 PM							
7:00 PM							
8:00 PM							
9:00 PM							
10:00 PM							
11:00 PM							
Midnight							

Putting It to **the Test**

If I had a dime for every student who reports test anxiety….

Some people really do suffer from true test anxiety, but the majority of students who claim to have this condition believe it to be true not because of an actual diagnosis, but rather because they get very nervous and may go blank during tests. By the end of a semester fewer students will raise their hands if asked if they have test anxiety. Why? They have learned how to take tests and how to stay calm. If you do suffer from test anxiety, consult with the counseling services at your school right away. Your advisor, or, at large schools, the person supervising introductory physics courses, can put you in contact with support services. You need to understand your condition and learn how to conquer it. The school where I teach offers classes three times a quarter for those whose anxiety can be helped by attending one or two sessions; your school might have a similar program.

Most people dread taking tests and experience some anxiety when taking them. Not surprisingly, the better prepared you are for an exam, the less worried you will be. The best remedy for the stress you associate with taking tests is to be very well prepared. If you know you understand the material, what is left to be worried about?

Some people get very anxious about tests because they fear they will not do well. For some it is because they know they are not prepared. The remedy is simple: Study well. But anxiety can also arise from a bad past experience. If you have done poorly on tests in the past, your self-confidence may be shot, so you anticipate doing poorly. That may lead to cramming and memorizing instead of real learning, and may cause you to become excessively nervous during the test. That, in turn, can cause poor performance. All you need to get your confidence back is a couple of good grades on tests.

Some experts recommend that test takers avoid studying for half an hour to an hour before an exam. Many students who complain of test anxiety frantically review their notes right up to the moment the test begins. By trying to look back over everything while racing against the clock, they are stressed when they begin the test. Remember that your brain needs time to process the information. When you cram information into the "closet," who knows what will fall out when you open the door during the test.

If you have studied well in advance and don't get very nervous at exam time, you might want to glance quickly at your notes beforehand, but only if you have time to do so and still allow *at least* a half hour to relax and prepare mentally for the test. The half hour off allows your brain to process the information while you relax. Try getting a light snack so you are alert. (A heavy meal could make you drowsy during the test.) Walk around to release nervous energy. Listen to music that makes you happy or calm. Sit comfortably, close your eyes, and breathe deeply and slowly while picturing yourself in a very relaxed setting, maybe a tropical beach, curled up on your couch with a good book, or out on a boat fishing. Focus on how relaxed you feel and try to hold on to that feeling. While remaining in that mood, concentrate on how well you have studied and keep reminding yourself of the following:

- I have prepared very well for this test.

- I know this material very well and I answered all questions correctly while studying.

- I can and *will* do well on this test.

- I refuse to get nervous over one silly test, especially because I know I am ready.

- I am ready and relaxed. Let's get it done!

Just don't become so relaxed you fall asleep and miss the test.

TEST-TAKING TIPS

There are a number of strategies you can use while taking a test. Let's see what your current strategies are. Complete the survey in Table 1.6. Then we will discuss specific strategies.

During an exam, be careful. Read each question thoroughly before you answer it. This is especially true of multiple choice and true-false questions. We know the answer is there, so our eyes tend to get ahead of our brains. We skim the question and jump down to the answers before even trying mentally to answer the question. Slow down and think so that you don't grab an answer that sounds correct or familiar, but is not

TABLE 1.6 **Self-evaluation of test-taking skills.** Indicate whether you use each of the following valuable test-taking skills always, sometimes, or never. Highlight any that you do not currently use that you think might help you to be more successful.

Test-taking Skills	Always	Sometimes	Never
1. While studying my notes and the book, I think of and answer any possible multiple choice questions.			
2. While studying my notes and the book, I think of and answer any possible problems.			
3. I use online practice quizzes and midterms when they are available.			
4. I avoid last-minute cramming to avoid confusing myself.			
5. I scan the whole test before starting to see how long it is and what types of questions it contains.			
6. I do the questions I am sure of first.			
7. I budget my time during a test so I can complete it.			
8. I answer questions with the highest point values first.			
9. I read all answer options on multiple choice questions before selecting an answer.			
10. I know what key words or concepts to look for in multiple choice questions.			
11. I use the process of elimination during multiple choice or matching tests.			
12. I look for key words like *always, never,* and *sometimes.*			
13. When I am unsure of an answer, I go with my first answer and fight the urge to change it later.			
14. I draw diagrams and list known and unknown quantities before solving a problem.			
15. I try to answer everything, even if I am uncertain, instead of leaving some questions blank.			
16. I check my answers, especially numerical calculations, before turning a test in.			

correct. If you can't avoid looking at the answers, cover them with your hand while you finish reading the question and thinking of the answer on your own. Of course, this doesn't work when the answers complete a sentence. In that case read each possibility carefully. In conceptual questions in physics, the distractors—the incorrect answers—are often based on preconceptions students bring with them to the class. These are the wrong answers you will jump to unless you are very careful. You will have a chance to check some of your preconceptions at the beginning of Chapter 3 and at the end of Chapter 4. Many of the exercises you will try in Chapters 3, 4, and 5 will help you engage with misleading common sense ideas.

If you do not know the answer initially, take a deep breath and think of all you do know about the words in the question. Often this is all you need to recall the answer. This is when prior work with concept maps may help you make the connections you need. Also use sketches and diagrams to help delineate physics problems.

In multiple choice problems, use the process of elimination. If you are not sure which answer is correct, can you eliminate any as incorrect? Narrow down your choices like contestants on the TV show *Who Wants to be a Millionaire?* (Wouldn't it be nice if you had lifelines!) If sure of the correct units or order of magnitude of the answer, you can eliminate choices with wrong units or of ridiculous orders of magnitude. Avoid making a guess unless the process of elimination fails you. However, guessing is usually better than leaving a question unanswered, unless you lose points for wrong answers. On short-answer or fill-in-the-blank questions, and in problem solving, always write something.

After you answer a question, read your answer to be sure it says what you want it to, then leave it alone. Once you move on, avoid the temptation to go back and change your answers, even those of which you were unsure. Often we have a gut instinct and write the correct answer; perhaps we are recalling it at some subconscious level. But the very act of going back is a conscious reminder of uncertainty, and we often choose something different only because we doubt ourselves.

When answering multiple choice or true-false questions, ignore any advice that you should select one answer consistently over others. Also, don't worry if you choose the same answer several times in a row. Most instructors don't give much thought to the pattern the answers will make on an answer sheet—I don't know any who do—so neither should you.

Here are a few more pointers:

■ Note the wording on questions. Key words to look for that can change an answer are *always, sometimes, never, most, some, all, none, is,* and *is not.*

- Glance over the exam as soon as you receive it, so you can know what to expect; then budget your time accordingly.

- Make sure you have received all pages of the exam.

- Look for questions on the backs of pages so you don't miss them.

- Tackle easy problems first. They may provide hints to the tougher ones.

- Be aware of point values and be sure the questions with the greatest point values are done well. Often problems to be solved, which usually are worth more points, are at the end, and some students run out of time before or while solving them. This results in a significant loss of points and seriously hurts their grades.

- If you have trouble solving problems, recall all you know that applies to that situation. Draw a sketch, write down the values of quantities you know, write down what you need to find, and turn your sketch into diagrams or graphs, if possible. Then recall the equations that connect the known and the unknown quantities, solve those equations for the unknown quantities, and then substitute numbers for symbols.

- If a problem has multiple parts, be sure to answer each part.

- If you are asked for a definition, give a book explanation of what the concept means. If you are asked for an example, list an example and explain why it is an example of the concept. Assume the reader has no prior knowledge so that you do not omit anything important.

- Be very thorough and specific in your answers. Do not leave out any algebraic steps. Do not solve the problem in your calculator and put down only the final answer. Show the final equation you are using before you substitute numbers in it. Do the substitution in writing on the page. The grader cannot read your mind, so you must put down every step.

- Finally, check your answers if there is time. Do they make sense? Are the units correct?

When a test is returned, record your grade. Be sure to review the test to see which questions and problems you missed, and why you missed them. Then make sure you understand that material thoroughly in case it appears on the final exam, or is needed for other tests before the final.

✔ **QUICK CHECK**

1. How can you slow yourself down when taking a multiple choice or true-false test?

_____

_____

2. How can you obtain maximum credit for problem solving?

_____

_____

Answers: 1. Cover the answers with your hand while you read the question, and don't look at them until you think of the answer. 2. Read the question carefully, sketch the situation, list knowns and unknowns, use diagrams or graphs as necessary, find equations that connect the known and unknown quantities, solve the equations, and substitute in numbers. Then check to be sure the answer is reasonable in magnitude and units.

Through the Looking Glass: **Individual Accountability**

I hope you have gained insight into the learning process and developed new strategies to improve your success, not just in physics, but in all of your classes. Last to consider, but not least, is your responsibility and attitude. When we get frustrated, we often look elsewhere for the cause, even when it may be right on our own shoulders. Poorly prepared students, with effort, may change into honors students, and honors students may drop out when they start getting really bad grades. Many factors, including insufficient math and physics preparation in high school, which this book is intended to partially overcome (truly inadequate preparation may take years to overcome), can contribute to poor grades. But especially for those who overcome their difficulties, a common thread among successful students is always attitude and accountability. Here are the facts you need to implant firmly in your mind:

1. **You,** and nobody else, chose to pursue this academic/career path.

2. **You,** and nobody else, are responsible for attaining the success you desire.

3. **You,** and nobody else, earn the grades you get.

You must do everything you can to guarantee your success. Nobody will do it for you. It has been said that how far a person will go is determined by that person's success at age 30. There are exceptions—such as late bloomers in the arts—but outstanding mathematicians and physicists tend to do their best work while still quite young. Those in other sciences typically get to wait longer, but you still need to work hard early in life if you are entering a scientific, medical, or engineering field.

That means always accepting responsibility for your own efforts. No excuses. To stay on track, you must know exactly what you want and always stay focused on where you are going. If you start to feel you can't keep up, don't quit or slack off. Focus on where you are going and why it matters to you. Always set short-term and long-term goals. Write them down and post them where you will see them often. You are responsible for keeping yourself motivated. Learn to visualize your success: See yourself in your future career. Think about how your life will be. Dream big. Then go after that dream with all you have.

An important part of the journey is to anticipate roadblocks before you hit them. Carefully think of any possible obstacles to your success, then plan around them. Do you have an unreliable car? Find someone you can ride to class with in emergencies. Do you have small children at home? Have daycare lined up and a backup plan for when your children are too ill to go to daycare. Do you have a learning disability? Immediately contact student support services or your counselor to find out what services are available to assist you. (A large school may have an Office of Disability Services.) Make a list of anything that might get between you and your success; then write down at least two possible solutions so you have a main strategy and a back-up plan.

Finally, consider those around you. Family and friends must know your goals and know how important they are to you. But do they support you? Perhaps your friends needle you because you don't go out as much, or you're no fun anymore. This can happen right in the dorm. Your significant other whines that you don't get enough time together or worries that, once you earn a degree, you won't need him or her anymore. Relatives accuse you of thinking you are better than they are because you are getting some education. Realize that when someone changes, whether through education or something else, those who know him or her may feel excluded, threatened, left behind, or even envious. You can try to assure them how much you still value and need them in your life, if you do, but don't let them distract you from your mission.

You must surround yourself with supportive people who are happy and proud of you, who celebrate your victories, and who want for you what you want. They will help you succeed. It may be your study group or others around you who will help you study. Perhaps they will watch your children so you can get some quiet time. On the other hand, anyone who ridicules you or is upset by your new schedule and goals is really not a friend you want around. Make new friends in class who share your goals and guard yourself from those who would derail you. Stay on track, and you will soon be living your dream. Good luck!

Final Stretch

Now that you have finished reading this chapter it is time to stretch your brain and check how much you have learned.

WHAT DID YOU LEARN?

In the following left-hand column, write your approach before reading this chapter. In the right-hand column, list any changes you plan to make to ensure your success in this class.

	What I have done before this chapter	**What I will do to improve**
During lectures:		
In recitation:		
In lab:		
Note taking:		
Textbook reading:		
My study place:		
Time management:		
Test taking:		

List three areas in which you think your study skills are the weakest, and ways in which you plan to improve them.

1.

2.

3.

WEB RESOURCES

Additional resources may be found online. Rather than giving specific Web addresses, which often change, even for the same material, the following suggestions will help you find both specific sites as well as alternate ones.

For this chapter, try entering the following headings in Google or any other search engine you are using:

Study Skills Inventory

Study Habit Inventory

Test-Taking Skills Survey

Exam Preparation

Concept Mapping

You will need to sort through the entries that appear. Because Google will list a very general article in Wikipedia first when you enter "Concept Mapping," you will need to work down to references that give specific advice. However, if you enter "Making Concept Maps," you will get a better list of more specific articles. By entering chapter section headings, you can get more information on those topics as well.

2 Using Math: Keep it in Proportion

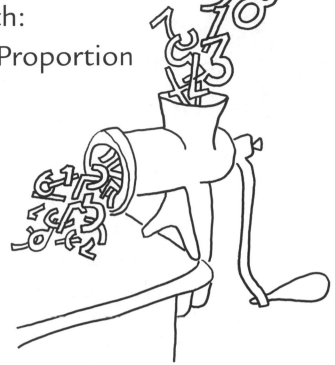

When you complete this chapter, you should be able to:

- Employ basic mathematical operations, traditionally or by use of a calculator.

- Solve simultaneous linear equations or quadratic equations.

- Simplify complex fractions.

- Use basic right-angle trigonometry.

- Work with logarithms and exponentials.

- Work with ratios and proportions of various kinds.

- Understand the use of significant figures, scientific notation, and useful prefixes.

- Be able to use vectors and calculate vector components.

- Construct graphs, and find the slope of a line and the area under a line.

Your Starting Point

Do You Still Remember These?

Answer the following questions to assess your basic math skills.

1. $\sqrt{100} =$ _____ or _____.

2. $x + 2 = 6.5; x =$ _____.

3. $\dfrac{1}{2} + \dfrac{1}{3} =$ _____.

4. $\left\{ \begin{array}{l} 2x + 3y = 3 \\ 3x + 2y = 7 \end{array} \right\}$ $x =$ _____, $y =$ _____.

5. $\dfrac{1}{p} + \dfrac{1}{4} = \dfrac{1}{2}; p =$ _____.

6. $PV = 18, V = 2; P =$ _____.

For 7 and 8, use Figure 2.1.

7. Leave in fraction form: $\cos\theta =$ _____.

8. Leave in fraction form: $\tan\theta =$ _____.

9. Solve $x^2 + x - 12 = 0$ for x; $x =$ _____ or $x =$ _____.

FIGURE 2.1 Triangle for questions 7 and 8.

10. Simplify $\dfrac{\dfrac{a-b}{1-ab}+b}{1+\dfrac{b(a-b)}{1-ab}}.$

Answers: 1. ∓10. 2. 4.5. 3. $\dfrac{6}{5}$. 4. $x = 3$, 5. $y = -1$, 6. $p = 9$.

7. $\cos\theta = \dfrac{5}{13}$. 8. $\tan\theta = \dfrac{12}{5}$. 9. $x = 3$ or -4. 10. a.

Math in Physics

An ancient Egyptian clay tablet on which a student was solving a word problem—incorrectly—has survived through the years to be found by archeologists. Science has depended on mathematical representations of physical phenomena ever since ancient societies observed the regularities in the motions of the sun, moon, and planets; began to predict eclipses and when to plant; and started to form theories of the nature of matter. Modern physics may be said to have begun when Pythagoras (born approximately 497 BCE) found a relationship between ratios of lengths of strings and consonant musical intervals. (The simpler the fraction expressing that ratio, the more harmonious the sound.) We could say that Pythagoras, who had observed the simple right triangles the ancient Egyptians used to divide arable farmland areas after the annual flooding of the Nile, had learned how to use *data* (results of experiments) to explain phenomena (natural occurrences). But note one thing: Pythagoras first played with string lengths and string tensions before arriving at the need for math.

Physics, the first of the sciences to isolate phenomena and so to obtain correspondences between numbers and physical quantities that could be varied controllably, found success by summarizing the data in laws, equations giving mathematical representations of physical regularities. This book is intended for two groups of students: those who plan to take the physics course for health science majors and those who plan to take the calculus-based physics course for engineering and other science majors. At some schools, all students take the calculus-based course. The good news is that if you possess the basic arithmetical skills—including adding, multiplying, dividing fractions, and working with least common denominators—you should be well equipped to tackle physics concepts. Much of first-year physics will involve working with proportional relationships, inverse as well as direct; fairly simple equations, linear and quadratic; and right-angle trigonometry. Only the electricity and magnetism part of the calculus-based course will make extensive use of calculus.

This chapter will include a quick review of basic arithmetical operations and will then concentrate on the math skills you need for either the algebra-trig or calculus-based physics courses.

Basic Math Operations

Calculators are both a blessing and a curse: blessing, because with a calculator you don't need to memorize many multiplication tables or do long divisions; curse, because through using a calculator you lose the ability to estimate whether or not an answer is correct from its magnitude.

I will assume that everyone knows how to use a calculator to obtain $28 \times 53 = 1484$ and also knows that $28 \times 53 = 53 \times 28$. (Both addition and multiplication are commutative. You can add or multiply a series of numbers in any order. But be careful with subtraction: $6 - 2 \neq 2 - 6$.) What you absolutely need to be able to do is recognize a wrong result if, without realizing it, you hit the divide button on the calculator instead of the multiply button.

WORKED EXAMPLE 2.1

For practice, estimate the result below *without* using a calculator:

$$\frac{(343)(587)}{(727)(296)} = \qquad\qquad \text{Eqn. 2.1}$$

Before you pick up a calculator to check, follow the reasoning here, which uses rounding:

$$\frac{(343)(587)}{(727)(296)} \approx \frac{(300)(600)}{(700)(300)} = \frac{6}{7} \approx 1$$

Because the exact answer of our modified example is 0.936, while $\frac{6}{7} = 0.857$, we see that our answer is within $\frac{0.857 - 0.936}{0.936} \times 100 = -8.4\%$ of the correct answer. This value, 8.4%, is the percent error of our estimate from the known value. The *deviation* is the difference 0.857 – 0.936, the result minus the known value. The *fractional error* is the deviation divided by the known value, and the percent error is the fractional error multiplied by 100.

Also note the following approach:

$\frac{343}{727} \approx \frac{1}{2}, \frac{587}{296} \approx 2$, so $\left(\frac{343}{727}\right) \times \left(\frac{587}{296}\right) \approx \left(\frac{1}{2}\right) \times 2 = 1$. No matter how we do the estimation, we can definitely find the order of magnitude of an answer, in other words, whether it is in single digits, 10s, 100s, and so on.

TIME TO TRY

Estimate

(a) $\frac{(222)(333)}{(555)(777)} =$

(b) $\frac{(8.574)(7.458)}{(3.672)} =$

(c) What method was used to simplify calculations in the previous estimates?

Answers: (a) $\left(\frac{2}{3}\right) \times \left(\frac{6}{8}\right) \approx \frac{1}{8} = 0.13$; the exact result is 0.17.

(b) $\frac{9 \cdot 7}{4} = \frac{63}{4} = \frac{60}{4} + \frac{3}{4} = 15.8$; the exact result is 17.4. (c) The numbers were rounded to one significant digit and zeroes, or estimated as simple fractions. This means we need to look more carefully at rounding and significant digits in a number.

ROUNDING

Not all measurements we make or numbers we calculate are meaningful. The number of digits we keep in a result are those within the margin of error. We call these *significant* figures. We will study rounding numbers here, and deal more extensively with significant figures and experimental errors later. For now, remember that significant figures do not include initial or ending zeroes that serve only to indicate the scale of a number.

✔ **QUICK CHECK**

Round the number 95168226 to

(a) 7 significant figures: _____.

(b) 6 significant figures: _____.

(c) 5 significant figures: _____.

(d) 4 significant figures: _____.

(e) 3 significant figures: _____.

Answers: (a) 95168230. (b) 95168200. (c) 95168000. (d) 95170000. (e) 95200000.

When rounding to six figures, 26 (formed by the last two digits) represents less than half of 100, so we round the last three digits down to 200. When rounding to four figures, 8226 (the last four digits) represents one-half or more of 10,000, so we round up to 95170000.

When do we round up, and when do we round down?

If the quantity to be rounded is 0% to 49% of the rightmost column that will keep a digit, don't change the number in that column (see [b] and [c]). If the quantity to be rounded is 50% or more of the number in the column being kept, increase that number by 1 (see [a], [d], and [e]).

SIGNIFICANT FIGURES To see why we need to round numbers consider how well you can measure a length with a ruler. How accurately can you measure liquids with a kitchen measuring cup? The smallest subdivisions on a ruler in centimeters are usually millimeters. You can estimate a length to about half a millimeter. A kitchen measuring cup is usually calibrated in ounces. You might be able to estimate a quantity to about a quarter of an ounce.

Use the following exercises to either review or acquaint yourself with how to determine and express significant figures. Pay particular attention to the rules determining the number of significant figures. The terms *accuracy* and *precision* will be illustrated in the following examples.

✔ **QUICK CHECK**

1. In a bio lab, a mite travels a distance of 4.7 cm (centimeters) in 3.00 s (seconds). What is its average speed?

2. You have counted scintillations in two separate experiments where the counts were limited to one-half hour to avoid eye strain. The first result was 5,824; the second was 6,017. What is the average number of scintillations per hour?

3. A result depends on the difference between 8,457 and 8,226. How many significant figures does the result have?

4. The result of an experiment depends on the difference between 5, 723, known to four significant figures, and 3, 550, known to three significant figures. How many significant figures are there in the result?

Answers: 1. The mite's average speed is $\dfrac{\text{distance}}{\text{time interval}} = \dfrac{4.7\ \text{cm}}{3.00\ \text{s}} = 1.6\ \dfrac{\text{cm}}{\text{s}}$. The answer a calculator gives, 1.566667 cm/s, is not correct, because the distance is only given to two digits. 2. The answer is the average of the two half-hour measurements (5,824 and 6,017) multiplied by 2. That comes out to the sum of the two counts, and is 11,841. However, $2 \times 5,824 = 11,648$ and $2 \times 6,017 = 12,034$. The first differs from the average counts per hour by $11,648 - 11,841 = -193$ and the second by $12,034 - 11,841 = +193$. This means that there is an uncertainty of ± 193 in the answer. Therefore, we round it off to $11,800 \pm 200$. The result 11,800 indicates the accuracy of the result. The error ± 200 indicates the precision. 3. Because $8,457 - 8,226 = 231$, there are only three significant figures in the result. 4. Because $5,723 - 3,550 = 2,173$ cannot have more significant figures than the number with the smaller number of significant figures, this should be rounded to 2,170 and have three significant figures.

When multiplying or dividing numbers, the answer only has as many significant digits as the number with the fewest digits. ■

The result of a sum is rounded to the column with the last significant digit in the number with the smallest number of significant figures. ■

When subtracting one number from another, the result will have no more significant figures than the number with the fewest significant figures. When one or more columns disappear(s) in the subtraction, the result has that many fewer significant figures. ■

Roughly, the total number of significant figures gives us the accuracy. The number to which the last significant figure, or last few significant figures, is known gives us the precision.

TIME TO TRY

An agribusiness quotes the number of egg-laying hens in its barns as 86,732 ± 110. How many significant figures should this number have?

Answer: There may be as many as 86,842 or as few as 86,622 hens in the barns. This number should be quoted as 86,700 ∓ 100 to convey a true account of the accuracy—three significant figures—and the precision, represented by the ∓100.

Use of Calculators

When calculating the answer to Equation 2.1, did you notice that as long as you hit the multiply key before entering 587 and the divide key before entering 727 or 296, the order didn't matter? That's one of the advantages in using a simple scientific calculator. The minimum calculator for most physics courses must add, subtract, multiply, and divide; square numbers and take square roots; provide sine, cosine, and tangent functions and inverse trig functions; give logs to base 10 and natural logarithms and their inverses; give exponentials and their inverses; and provide y^x and $y^{1/x}$ functions. If the calculator has a special key for π, that's useful, but not necessary. (If you have had a math course that required a more complicated calculator with parentheses having to be entered, etc., be sure you mastered its use.) ■

MULTIPLE OPERATIONS

Determine the solution to the following multiple operation problem.

$$\text{The value of } 81 - \left[\frac{(28)(4 - x)}{7} \right] \text{ when } x + 5 = 7 \text{ is } \underline{\hspace{2cm}}.$$

The easiest way to solve this is to find $x = 7 - 5 = 2$, and then solve $81 - \left[\frac{(28)(4 - 2)}{7} \right]$. Note that the order in which operations are performed is important. Start with the innermost parentheses and work outward:

$$4 - 2 = 2$$
$$28(2) = 56$$
$$\frac{56}{7} = 8$$
$$81 - 8 = 73$$

Alternatively,

$$4 - 2 = 2$$
$$\frac{28}{7} = 4$$
$$4 \cdot 2 = 8$$
$$81 - 8 = 73$$

Order of Multiple Operations

1. Do all operations inside parentheses or brackets first. Work from the innermost to the outermost parentheses.

2. Do all multiplications and divisions in each term in the order previously indicated.

3. Finally, add and subtract the terms as indicated by their signs. ■

CANCELLATION

Is the following cancellation correct? $\dfrac{64}{16} = \dfrac{\cancel{6}4}{1\cancel{6}} = 4$. Right? WRONG! Although the answer is correct, the result is accidental, as we see from $\dfrac{3\cancel{2}}{\cancel{2}} = 3$, which is obviously wrong because $2 \times 16 = 32$. You can't cancel digits within numbers, only entire numbers for which the complete sets of digits cancel.

TIME TO TRY

Simplify the following fraction by canceling numbers where possible:

$$\frac{(537)(60)}{(15)(537)} = \underline{\hspace{2cm}}.$$

Answer: $\dfrac{(537)(60)}{(15)(537)} = \dfrac{(1)(60)}{(15)} = 4$

Scientific Notation

Scientists and workers in scientific fields must be able to communicate without ambiguity. A difference of a factor of ten in a heart medication may be the difference between life and death for a patient. Scientific notation removes all ambiguity in numbers.

For instance, what is the difference between 3,330, 3,330., and 3,330.0? The implication is that we know 3330. to four decimal places, and 3,330.0 to five, but 3330 could be accurate to one, two, three, or four places. To remove any such uncertainty, we place a decimal point after the first digit, add all other digits that are known to be accurate, and multiply by a power of 10 to correct for the decimal placement. This method of expression is called scientific notation.

✔ **QUICK CHECK**

1. If 53,353 is known to five significant figures, express it in scientific notation.

2. Express 8,275,000 m in scientific notation. Only the first four digits are known to be accurate.

3. Express 0.00287 in scientific notation.

Answers: 1. It should be 5.3353×10^4. Note that the exponent in 10^4 tells how many decimal places to the left the decimal point has been moved. 2. This is 8.275×10^6. We drop the place-holder zeroes when they contain no information about the accuracy or precision of the number. 3. This is 2.87×10^{-3}. Here the 0.00 only gives the decimal order of magnitude—the power of ten—of the number. We never write 0002.87×10^{-3}, because the initial zeroes are meaningless.

Note that scientific notation is easy to work with if you understand the rules for exponents. (See Laws of Exponents on pages 100–101.)

COMMON PREFIXES

Some decimal orders of magnitude, particular powers of 10, occur so often that they are indicated by prefixes. Table 2.1 gives a list of these. You will encounter others later in science courses, but the ones given in the table should be memorized. That will give you a good head start so you won't use the wrong power of ten when converting micrograms or milligrams to grams.

TABLE 2.1 The most common decimal prefixes.

Prefix	Symbol	Decimal Equivalent	Exponential Equivalent
giga	G	1,000,000,000	10^9
mega	M	1,000,000	10^6
kilo	k	1,000	10^3
deka	D	10	10^1
		1	10^0
demi	d	0.1	10^{-1}
centi	c	0.01	10^{-2}
milli	m	0.001	10^{-3}
micro	μ	0.000 001	10^{-6}
nano	n	0.000 000 001	10^{-9}
pico	p	0.000 000 000 001	10^{-12}

✔ **QUICK CHECK**

Refer to Table 2.1.

1. What is a deciliter?

2. What is a megavolt?

Answers: 1. A deciliter is 10^{-1} liter, or one-tenth of a liter. 2. A megavolt is 10^6 volts, or one million volts.

Algebra

SIMULTANEOUS LINEAR EQUATIONS

WORKED EXAMPLE 2.2

Given $\begin{cases} 8x - 5y = 28 \\ -3x + 6y = 6 \end{cases}$, solve for x and y.

The basic technique for solving simultaneous linear equations is to multiply each equation by a number such that either the terms in x or the terms in y sum to zero. Here

$\begin{cases} 3[8x - 5y] = 3(28) \\ 8[-3x + 6y] = 8(6) \end{cases}$ so

$\begin{cases} 24x - 15y = 84 \\ -24x + 48y = 48 \end{cases}$ and $0 + 33y = 132$, with $y = 4$.

Substitute the value of y in either equation to find x:

$$8x - 5(4) = 28$$
$$8x = 48$$
$$x = 6$$

Solve the same two simultaneous equations by eliminating y:

Answer: Use $\begin{aligned} 6[8x - 5y] = 6(28) \\ 5[-3x + 6y] = 5(6) \end{aligned}$

> Warning: If one equation is a multiple of the other equation, we have only one equation and cannot solve it.
>
> Example: $2x + 3y = 5$ and $4x + 6y = 10$ are the same equation because the second equation is the first one multiplied by 2.

✔ QUICK CHECK

Solve for x and y:

1. $\begin{cases} 5x + 2y = 6 \\ 3x + 4y = 12 \end{cases}$

Solve for I_1, I_2, and I_3:

2. $\begin{cases} 2I_1 + 3I_2 - 6I_3 = 4 \\ 4I_1 - 2I_2 + 4I_3 = 8 \\ I_1 + I_2 - 4I_3 = 1 \end{cases}$

Note: Equations like these can arise when solving Kirchoff's laws for currents, I, in multi-loop resistive circuits. This example also illustrates the fact that we use many different symbols in physics, which makes it difficult to recognize math that we already know. That issue will be addressed later in this chapter.

Answers: 1. $x = 0$, $y = 3$. 2. $I_1 = 2$, $I_2 = 1$, $I_3 = \dfrac{1}{2}$. (Quick Check example 2 can be solved by the same method as Quick Check example 1, by eliminating one unknown quantity first, and then a second one, to be able to solve for the third unknown quantity.)

QUADRATIC EQUATIONS

Remember that quadratic equations are equations that contain the square of a quantity. Equations of the form $ax^2 = b$ are trivial because $x = \pm\sqrt{\dfrac{b}{a}}$. Therefore, we will review equations of the form $ax^2 + bx + c = 0$.

Some quadratic equations can be factored fairly easily into the form $(x - p)(x - q) = 0$. Solve $x^2 - 7x + 12 = 0$ for x: $x = $ _____ or _____ .

If you notice that $4 + 3 = 7$ and $4 \times 3 = 12$, you can see that $x^2 - 7x + 12 = (x - 3)(x - 4) = 0$ so $x = 3$ or $x = 4$. (Because either factor may be zero, either factor yields a solution to the equation.)

Write any quadratic equation in the form $ax^2 + bx + c = 0$ and divide by a. We now have $(1)x^2 + b'x + c' = 0$. The previous example showed that $b' = -(p + q)$ and $c' = +pq$. When p and q are small integers, it is often possible to see what they are by inspecting b' and c'. ∎

When you cannot find the solution by inspection, you must use the quadratic formula:

$$x = \frac{-b \pm \sqrt{b^2 - 4ac}}{2a}.$$

✔ QUICK CHECK

1. Solve $x^2 + 3x - 10 = 0$ for x.

2. Solve for x: $x^2 + 4x - 21 = 0$.

3. Solve for t: $4t^2 - 16t + 15 = 0$.

4. Solve $2x^2 + 8x + 6 = 0$ by the quadratic formula.

Answers: 1. Because this is the same as $(x + 5)(x - 2) = 0$, $x = -5$ or $x = 2$.

2. $x = 3$, $x = -7$. 3. $t = \frac{3}{2}$, $t = \frac{7}{2}$. 4. $x = \frac{-8 \pm \sqrt{64 - 4(12)}}{4} =$

$= \frac{-8 \mp \sqrt{64 - 48}}{4} = \frac{-8 \mp \sqrt{16}}{4} = \frac{-8 \mp 4}{4}$, so $x = -3$ or $x = -1$. In

factored form this equation is $2(x + 1)(x + 3) = 0$.

In 4, did you note that all the terms were multiples of 2, so the equation could have been simplified to $x^2 + 4x + 3 = 0$? Always look for ways of simplifying what you have to solve.

TIME TO TRY

1. Solve for ω: $9\omega^2 = 25$. (The Greek letter ω, omega, often represents angular velocity.)

2. Solve for t: $4t^2 - 2t - 6 = 0$. (The letter t usually represents time.)

3. Solve for x: $x^2 - 9abx + 20a^2b^2 = 0$. (This example illustrates the fact that equations may include symbols as well as numbers. In physics these may be well-known symbols, such as that for the speed of light. We can then insert numbers in the solution to replace the symbols.)

Answers: 1. $\omega = \mp\dfrac{5}{3}$. 2. $t = -1$ or $t = \dfrac{3}{2}$. 3. $x = 4ab$ or $x = 5ab$.

It's worth memorizing the quadratic formula even though many calculators are set up to solve quadratic equations. You should keep in mind that if you are in a class where you are not allowed to use alphanumeric calculators or preprogrammed solutions, this one formula will be very useful. And you can then use it to check that you entered the constants in your calculator correctly. ■

More Complex Operations

COMMON DENOMINATORS

When asked to find a common denominator for two fractions, most students can do it. However, when the need to do so arises in the course of a physics problem, many students are unable to continue because the knowledge is compartmentalized as "math," not "science." (This stumbling block was already mentioned in the second practice exercise.) Keep this in mind when you have to add or subtract fractions in a physics problem. Remember, "Common denom is a known phenom (enon.)"

Try another example: Add $\dfrac{1}{3} + \dfrac{1}{4} = $ _____ .

First multiply each number by 1, so $\frac{1}{3}(1) + \frac{1}{4}(1) =$ _____. Then multiply $\frac{1}{3}$ by $\frac{4}{4}$ in place of 1 and multiply $\frac{1}{4}$ by $\frac{3}{3}$ in place of 1.

This results in $\frac{1}{3}\left(\frac{4}{4}\right) + \frac{1}{4}\left(\frac{3}{3}\right) = \frac{4}{12} + \frac{3}{12} = \frac{7}{12}$.

In this process each denominator became $3 \times 4 = 12$. Alternatively, you can multiply the two denominators together to get a common denominator and multiply each numerator by the other fraction's denominator. Use whichever method works for you.

Now try this with symbols rather than numbers: $\frac{1}{a} + \frac{1}{b} =$ _____.

Answer: $\frac{1b}{ab} + \frac{1a}{ba} = \frac{a + b}{ab}$

✔ QUICK CHECK

1. $\frac{1}{3} - \frac{1}{4} =$ _____.

2. $\frac{1}{a} - \frac{1}{b} =$ _____.

3. $\frac{5}{6} - \frac{2}{3} =$ _____.

4. $\frac{3}{p} + \frac{5}{q} =$ _____.

5. $\frac{p}{q^2} - \frac{2q}{p} =$ _____.

Answers: 1. $\frac{1}{12}$. 2. $\frac{b-a}{ab}$. 3. $\frac{1}{6}$. 4. $\frac{5q+3p}{pq}$. 5. $\frac{p^2-2q^3}{pq^2}$.

SIMPLIFYING COMPLEX FRACTIONS

See if you remember how to divide one fraction by another. Simplify:

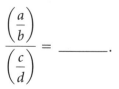

$$\frac{\left(\dfrac{a}{b}\right)}{\left(\dfrac{c}{d}\right)} = \underline{\qquad}.$$

Here it is best to use a general formula before proceeding to specific cases and rules:

$$\frac{\left(\dfrac{a}{b}\right)}{\left(\dfrac{c}{d}\right)} = \frac{\left(\dfrac{a}{b}\right)\left(\dfrac{b}{1}\right)}{\left(\dfrac{c}{d}\right)\left(\dfrac{b}{1}\right)} = \frac{\left(\dfrac{a}{1}\right)}{\left(\dfrac{cb}{d}\right)} = \frac{\left(\dfrac{a}{1}\right)\left(\dfrac{d}{1}\right)}{\left(\dfrac{cb}{d}\right)\left(\dfrac{d}{1}\right)} = \frac{\left(\dfrac{ad}{1}\right)}{\left(\dfrac{bc}{1}\right)}.$$

Because anything divided by one is equal to itself, $\dfrac{ad}{1} = ad$ and $\dfrac{bc}{1} = bc$. Finally,

$$\frac{\left(\dfrac{a}{b}\right)}{\left(\dfrac{c}{d}\right)} = \frac{ad}{bc}.$$

But this is the same result you would get by multiplying $\dfrac{a}{b}$ by $\dfrac{d}{c}$ instead of dividing it by $\dfrac{c}{d}$.

 The rule for dividing fractions is to invert the fraction in the denominator (bottom) first, and then multiply the fraction in the numerator (top) by this inverted fraction. ■

✔ **QUICK CHECK**

1. $\dfrac{\dfrac{2}{5}}{\dfrac{8}{7}} = $ _____ .

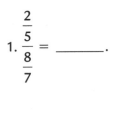

Answer: 1. $\dfrac{\dfrac{2}{5}}{\dfrac{8}{7}} = \dfrac{2}{5} \times \dfrac{7}{8} = \dfrac{14}{40} = \dfrac{7}{20}$

All difficulties in simplifying fractions vanish if you pay close attention to parentheses and find common denominators as needed. But you will also need to know how to divide one fraction by another.

Simplify
$$
\dfrac{1 - \dfrac{\dfrac{2}{3} + \dfrac{1}{4}}{\dfrac{1}{3} - \dfrac{1}{4}}}{1 + \dfrac{\dfrac{2}{3} - \dfrac{1}{4}}{\dfrac{1}{3} + \dfrac{1}{4}}} = \underline{\qquad}.
$$

You may want to say "forget it!" if it's been a while since complex fractions were taken up in a math class. However, go as far as you can by using the rule in the previous key statement before checking with the following step-by-step solution.

First, note the implied parentheses and brackets:

$$
\dfrac{1 - \dfrac{\dfrac{2}{3} + \dfrac{1}{4}}{\dfrac{1}{3} - \dfrac{1}{4}}}{1 + \dfrac{\dfrac{2}{3} - \dfrac{1}{4}}{\dfrac{1}{3} + \dfrac{1}{4}}} = \dfrac{1 - \left[\dfrac{\left(\dfrac{2}{3} + \dfrac{1}{4}\right)}{\left(\dfrac{1}{3} - \dfrac{1}{4}\right)}\right]}{1 + \left[\dfrac{\left(\dfrac{2}{3} - \dfrac{1}{4}\right)}{\left(\dfrac{1}{3} + \dfrac{1}{4}\right)}\right]}.
$$

By finding common denominators we obtain

$$
\dfrac{1 - \left[\dfrac{\dfrac{11}{12}}{\dfrac{1}{12}}\right]}{1 + \left[\dfrac{\dfrac{5}{12}}{\dfrac{7}{12}}\right]} = \dfrac{1 - 11}{1 + \dfrac{5}{7}} = \dfrac{-10}{\dfrac{12}{7}} = \dfrac{-70}{12} = \dfrac{-35}{6}.
$$

1. $\dfrac{\dfrac{1}{a^2} - \dfrac{1}{b^2}}{\dfrac{1}{a} - \dfrac{1}{b}} = $ _____.

2. $\dfrac{\dfrac{1+x}{1-x} - x}{1 + \dfrac{x(1+x)}{1-x}} = $ _____.

Answers 1. $\dfrac{a+b}{ab}$. 2. $+1$.

PROPORTIONS

PICTURE THIS

Owing to the economic downturn, a school has been forced to cancel the band for the senior prom unless the students can raise the money themselves for the band. To do this, some students plan on having a bake sale. A cookbook states that a basic puff pastry recipe of 2 cups of flour and $\frac{1}{2}$ pound of unsalted butter will make 60 palm cookies (also called elephant ears). The students want to make 510 cookies.

How many cups of flour will they need? How many pounds of butter will they need?

A ratio is a comparison between two numbers, usually written as $a{:}b$ or $\dfrac{a}{b}$. Our ratio of flour to cookies is $\dfrac{2 \text{ cups flour}}{60 \text{ cookies}}$ and of butter to cookies is $\dfrac{\frac{1}{2} \text{ cup butter}}{60 \text{ cookies}}$. In this recipe, the ratio of butter to flour, $\dfrac{\frac{1}{2} \text{ cup butter}}{2 \text{ cups flour}}$, remains the same no matter how many cookies you make.

If the students need 2 cups of flour for 60 cookies, then they need an unknown number of cups, x, for 510 cookies, but the amount of flour for each cookie is the same. "For each" is sometimes written as "per," and we can then say that the amount of flour "per" cookie is the same. Thus, $\dfrac{2 \text{ cups flour}}{60 \text{ cookies}} = \dfrac{x}{510 \text{ cookies}}$ and

$x = \dfrac{1020}{60}$ cups of flour $= 17$ cups of flour. An equality of two ratios, such as $\dfrac{2 \text{ cups flour}}{60 \text{ cookies}} = \dfrac{x}{510 \text{ cookies}}$ is called a proportion.

To find the number of cups of butter that the students will need, we use the same method:

The proportion is $\dfrac{\frac{1}{2} \text{ cup butter}}{60 \text{ cookies}} = \dfrac{x}{510 \text{ cookies}}$, so $x = \dfrac{255}{60}$ pounds of butter $= 4.25$ pounds of butter.

Note: this example has been kept simple by omitting the third ingredient, salt, and the details of preparation. Check a cookbook, not a physics book, to make cookies.

WORKED EXAMPLE 2.3

1. If a department store sells 187 pairs of men's socks in a week, how many pairs must the buyer order each year?

   Use the proportion $\dfrac{187}{1} = \dfrac{x}{52}$. Then $x = 52 \times 187 = 9{,}724$ pairs of socks. Note that this should be rounded to 9.72×10^3 in scientific notation because 52 is an absolute number and 187 has three significant figures.

2. Because class sizes vary from very small to very large, a university building committee uses a rule of thumb that one classroom is needed for each 25 students. How many classrooms are needed for 1,200 students?

Use the proportion $\frac{1}{25} = \frac{x}{12,000}$, so $x = 480$ classrooms.

3. The same university committee also follows a rule that they need one large classroom for every seven small classrooms. How many small classrooms does this 1,200-student university have?

Let s stand for the number of small classrooms and ℓ stand for the number of large classrooms. From (2) we already know that $s + \ell = 480$. From the information in this problem we know that $\frac{\ell}{s} = \frac{1}{7}$. Therefore, $s + \frac{s}{7} = 480$ and $s = \frac{3360}{8} = 420$. (Write out the missing intermediate step between the last two equations for practice.) That means $\ell = 480 - s = 480 - 420 = 60$. Alternatively, we could have solved $\ell + 7\ell = 480$ to find $\ell = 60$ directly, and then have found s. Would you have read the harder first method if we had started with the easier alternative method? Possibly, but keep in mind that it's always better to understand all possible problem-solving methods.

TIME TO TRY

These problems illustrate more abstract situations where symbols stand for invisible atoms or for general numbers.

1. There are twice as many hydrogen atoms as oxygen atoms in any quantity of water, H_2O. If there are 270,000 molecules of water in a test tube, how many hydrogen atoms does it contain?

2. A proportion can be written symbolically as $\frac{a}{b} = \frac{c}{d}$. Show that $\frac{b}{a} = \frac{d}{c}$.

Answers: 1. Let h stand for the number of hydrogen atoms and w for the number of water molecules. Then, $\frac{h}{w} = \frac{2}{1}$. But $w = 270,000$, so $h = 270,000 \cdot 2 = 540,000$ hydrogen atoms. 2. Multiply the numerators by the product of the denominators: $\frac{a}{b}(bd) = \frac{c}{d}(bd)$, so $ad = bc$. Now divide by ac, the product of the original numerators: $\frac{ad}{ac} = \frac{bc}{ac}$, so $\frac{d}{c} = \frac{b}{a}$, which is the same as $\frac{b}{a} = \frac{d}{c}$.

DIRECT PROPORTIONS When we have a simple equation such as that for the number of cups of flour, c, as a function of the number of cookies, N, we can write $\frac{1}{30} = \frac{c}{N}$ or $c = \frac{1}{30}N$. When an unknown, or dependent quantity, c, is a simple multiple of a known, or independent, quantity, N, we have a direct proportion. No matter what symbols are used, this is always represented in the form $y = ax$ where the value of y depends on the value of x multiplied by a constant a. Note that the equation of a straight line, $y = mx + b$, is a direct proportion only when $b = 0$. When $b \neq 0$, we have a linear relationship, but not a direct proportion.

✔ **QUICK CHECK**

Which of the following are direct proportions and which are linear relationships? Look at the form of the equations: the symbols represent physical quantities. Also note that x and y are used in physics for representations of position along a coordinate axis.

1. $v = v_0 + at$. (v and t are variables, v_0 and a are constants.)

2. $v_{\text{tang}} = \omega r$. ($v_{\text{tang}}$ and ω are variables, r is a constant.)

3. $S = \dfrac{E^2}{c}$. (S and E are variables, c is a constant.)

Answers: 1. Linear relationship (it is of the form $y = b + mx$). 2. Direct proportion. 3. Direct proportion (S is proportional to the quantity E^2 rather than to E).

THE GOLDEN MEAN When the proportion between three quantities is such that $\dfrac{a}{b} = \dfrac{b}{c}$, then b is the "golden mean" between a and c. This ratio occurs in nature and is used by artists and architects, among others.

CONTINUED PROPORTIONS Suppose a car drives 44 miles on 1.6 gallons of gas. How many gallons should the gas tank hold if the car is to be able to drive 330 miles without stopping for gas? We need to know how many miles the car gets to the gallon to be able to determine how many gallons it needs to travel 330 miles.

This calculation involves two steps. You will have to solve many problems that involve more than one step. Many students want to be able to look for the equation that solves the problem, but physics is about how you solve problems when you do not know the answer ahead of time. Study this problem carefully. It is a very simple example of the sort of solution that is needed frequently.

We first set up a proportion to find the miles per gallon: $\dfrac{44 \text{ mi}}{1.6 \text{ gal}} = \dfrac{x}{1 \text{ gal}}$, so $x = 27.5 \dfrac{\text{mi}}{\text{gal}}$. Then we follow with a second proportion: $\dfrac{1 \text{ gal}}{27.5 \text{ mi}} = \dfrac{y}{330 \text{ mi}}$, so $y = 12$ gal. This illustrates how the result of one proportion may become the basic information used for solving another proportion. Similarly, the solution of one linear or other equation may become the input of another equation. After you become used to such problems, you will be able to omit the intermediate step and immediately write $\dfrac{1.6 \text{ gal}}{44 \text{ mi}} = \dfrac{y}{330 \text{ mi}}$.

WORKED EXAMPLE 2.4

Let's apply this approach to another situation. You are riding in a long railroad car that is moving at a constant velocity of $10 \dfrac{\text{m}}{\text{s}}$ (meter per second = meters covered in each second of movement). You start at the midpoint of the car and run backward relative to the car at $0.5 \dfrac{\text{m}}{\text{s}}$ for 5.0 s. Your friend starts at the same point but runs forward at $0.5 \dfrac{\text{m}}{\text{s}}$.

1. How far have you moved relative to the ground outside at the end of 5.0 s?

   The train moves 10 m in one second, so it moves 50 m in 5.0 seconds (proportional reasoning). You move $\left(0.5 \dfrac{\text{m}}{\text{s}} \right)(5.0 \text{ s}) = 2.5 \text{ m}$ backward. Therefore, relative to the ground outside you moved 50 m forward and 2.5 m backward, or 47.5 m forward.

2. How far has your friend moved relative to the ground outside at the end of 5.0 s?

   The answer is reached similarly to (a), but your friend moves 50 m + 2.5 m = 52.5 m forward relative to the ground outside.

3. How far apart are you and your friend at that time, according to another passenger in the train?

You each moved 2.5 m away from the center, so you are 5.0 m apart.

4. How far apart are you and your friend, according to an observer looking in from a station platform as the train passes by?

The person outside also sees you as 5.0 m apart. When the person looks in the windows of the train at the end of the 5.0 s time interval, she sees exactly where you are in the train. Imagine that meters are indicated on the station platform. Then she can read your positions and determine how far apart you are.

INVERSE PROPORTIONS We have an inverse proportion when the product of two quantities remains constant even though the quantities themselves vary. For a fixed voltage drop V_0 across varying resistance R, the current I in the circuit is always such that $IR = V_0$. Because V_0 is constant, we write this as $I = \dfrac{V_0}{R}$. In notation you might see in a math class it would be written as $y = \dfrac{c}{x}$, where x varies independently and c is a constant.

Graphs

When you start to solve physics problems, you will be encouraged to use several different methods for representing the information. A picture that shows positions of objects in initial and final states is usually very helpful. Because we model objects as point particles, you will then produce a simplified picture: a diagrammatic representation. When you have sufficient data or equations, you may find that a graph is the best representation to use.

GRAPHS OF DIRECT PROPORTIONS AND LINEAR RELATIONSHIPS

Graphs can represent linear relationships between variables, including direct proportions.

WORKED EXAMPLE 2.5

As you solve these examples, remember that a *y*-intercept on a graph is the value of *y* when $x = 0$.

1. Graph $y = 2x$ on the axes in Figure 2.2.

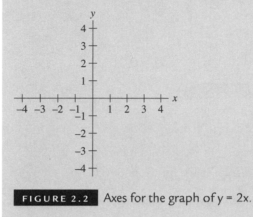

FIGURE 2.2   Axes for the graph of $y = 2x$.

This is a direct proportion. Because *y* is a constant times *x* for any direct proportion, no matter what *x* and *y* represent, the graph of a direct proportion always goes through the origin.

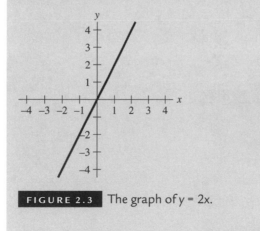

FIGURE 2.3   The graph of $y = 2x$.

2. Graph $y = 2x - 1$ on the axes in Figure 2.4.

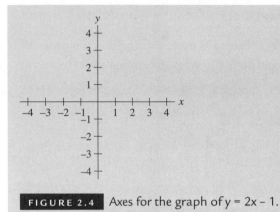

FIGURE 2.4   Axes for the graph of $y = 2x - 1$.

This is a graph of a straight line, but not a direct proportion. The ratio $\dfrac{y}{x}$ is not constant because $\dfrac{y}{x} = 2 - \dfrac{1}{x}$. The added constant –1 displaces the line from the origin so it has a y-intercept of –1.

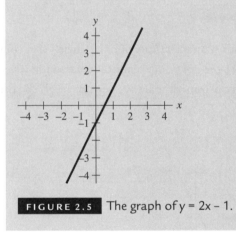

FIGURE 2.5   The graph of $y = 2x - 1$.

TIME TO TRY

1. Graph $y = -3x$.

2. Graph $y = -3x + 2$.

values (values of y when $x = 0$).

The lines in (1) and (2) have the same slopes and make the same angle with the x-axis, but they cross the y-axis at different points. They have different y-intercept

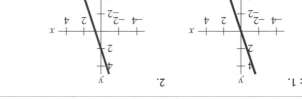
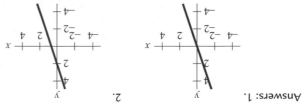
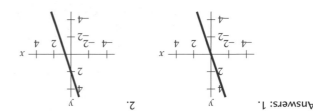

Answers: 1.   2.

The equation of a direct proportion $y = cx$ is a straight line through the origin. The equation of a straight line that does not go through the origin has the form $y = mx + b$, where m is the slope and b is the y-intercept. A direct proportion is a special case of a linear relationship because $b = 0$. ∎

WORKED EXAMPLE 2.6

1. Find the slope of the line in the graph in Figure 2.6.

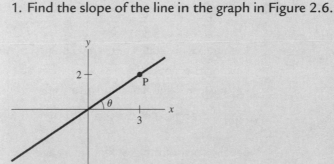

FIGURE 2.6 Graph of a line through the points (0,0) and (3,2).

To find the slope, we pick any two points sufficiently far apart on the line. For this line we know the coordinates of two points, the origin (0,0), and the point (3,2). In this notation, 3 stands for the x-coordinate and 2 for the y-coordinate. The slope, usually symbolized by the letter m, is given by the difference in the y-coordinates divided by the difference in the x-coordinates. We can call it the "rise," $\Delta y = y_A - y_B$, over the "run," $\Delta x = x_A - x_B$, for any two points A and B. The Greek letter Δ, "delta," applied to any symbol instructs us to take the difference of its values at two different points. Thus

$$m = \frac{\Delta y}{\Delta x} = \frac{y_P - y_O}{x_P - x_O} = \frac{2 - 0}{3 - 0} = \frac{2}{3}.$$

2. Find the slope of the line in the graph in Figure 2.7.

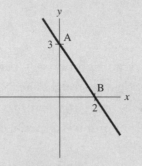

FIGURE 2.7   Graph of a line through the point (0,3) and (2,0).

We calculate the slope the same way we did in (1):

$$m = \frac{\Delta y}{\Delta x} = \frac{y_A - y_B}{x_A - x_B} = \frac{3 - 0}{0 - 2} = -\frac{3}{2}.$$ Note how important it is to keep the coordinates of the two points in the correct order when calculating the slope. Because y increases as x decreases and becomes negative, this line has a negative slope.

3. Find the angle θ in the graph shown in worked example (1).

See the copy of the graph in Figure 2.8.

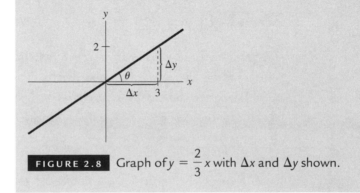

FIGURE 2.8   Graph of $y = \frac{2}{3}x$ with Δx and Δy shown.

The vertical dashed line is Δy, and the horizontal dashed line is Δx. But they are also the opposite and adjacent, respectively, for the angle θ. Therefore, $\tan \theta = \dfrac{OPP}{ADJ} = \dfrac{\Delta y}{\Delta x} = \dfrac{2}{3}$. This is the slope of the line.

The slope is the tangent of the angle the line makes with the x-axis. We can use our calculators to find $\tan^{-1}\left(\dfrac{2}{3}\right) = 33.7°$.

On any straight line, pick any two points sufficiently far apart and find the ratio of the differences in their y- and x-values: that is the slope $m = \dfrac{\Delta y}{\Delta x} = \dfrac{y_A - y_B}{x_A - x_B}$. The slope is also the tangent of the angle the line makes with the x-axis. ■

Trigonometry is reviewed later in this chapter.

AREA UNDER A GRAPH

The area under the curve in a graph often has a direct physical meaning. For instance, the area under a graph of velocity versus time represents the displacement of an object. For this reason it is important to be able to calculate the area under any such graph.

WORKED EXAMPLE 2.7

1. What is the area under the graph shown in Figure 2.9, from $x = 0$ to $x = 6$?

   The area is a triangle with the origin at one vertex, the point (6,0) at another vertex, and the point (6,4) at the third vertex. The area of a triangle is one-half the base times the height. Because this is a right triangle, the height is the right side of the triangle from (6,0) to (6,4), or 4 units of length. The base is the distance from the origin to (6,4), or 6 units of length. Therefore, $A = \dfrac{1}{2}bh = \dfrac{1}{2}(6) \cdot (4) = 12$.

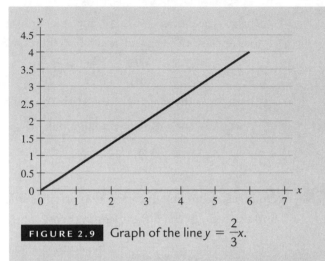

FIGURE 2.9   Graph of the line $y = \dfrac{2}{3}x$.

2. Compute the area under the graph in Figure 2.10 from $x = 0$ to $x = 4$.

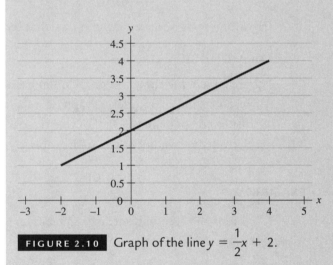

FIGURE 2.10   Graph of the line $y = \dfrac{1}{2}x + 2$.

The area between this line and the *x*-axis consists of a triangle with vertices (0,2), (4,2), and (4,4) and a rectangle with vertices (0,0), (0,2), (4,2), and (4,0). Draw the triangle and the rectangle in the figure. Can you see that the area of the triangle is $A = \dfrac{1}{2}(4) \cdot (2) = 4$ and that the area of the rectangle is $A = (4) \cdot (2) = 8$ so that the total area under the line is 12 units of area?

3. What is the area under the graph in Figure 2.11, from $x = 0$ to $x = 4$?

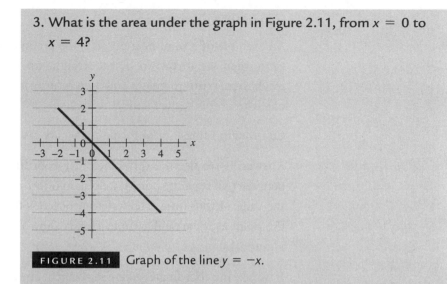

FIGURE 2.11   Graph of the line $y = -x$.

Here the line extends below the x-axis and the triangle has vertices (0,0), (4,0), and (4,–4). Therefore the area is $A = \frac{1}{2}bh = \frac{1}{2}(4) \cdot (-4) =$ –8 units of area. Remember that our base is $\Delta x = x_{(4,0)} - x_{(0,0)} = 4$, but our height is $\Delta y = y_{(4,-4)} - y_{(4,0)} = -4$. Can you show that the angle between the line and the x-axis is $-45°$?

GRAPHS PROPORTIONAL TO A POWER OF A QUANTITY

We often encounter relationships where the dependent quantity is proportional to or linearly related to a power of another quantity. Examples are electric power proportional to resistance times the square of the current ($P = RI^2$); the probability per unit length of finding a particle at the point x on the x-axis in quantum mechanics, which is proportional to the square of the normalized wave function $\psi(x)$: $P = |\psi(x)|^2$; and kinetic energy, which is equal to one-half the mass of a particle times its velocity squared ($K = \frac{1}{2}mv^2$). These examples also illustrate a danger: because the alphabet is limited, the same letter symbol sometimes has to represent more than one concept. Here P stand for power in one example and for probability density—probability per unit length—in another.

NONLINEAR GRAPHS

An example of a nonlinear graph is the graph of vertical height versus time when we throw an object straight up into the air. The object reaches a maximum height and then returns to your hand. An example of such a graph is given in Figure 2.12.

Can you find the slope at the points where t is 1, 2, 3, 4, and 5 seconds?

Answer: If we use the difference in y-coordinates and t-coordinates between two separate points, we obtain only a sort of average value, not the value at that time. The way to proceed is to draw a line tangent to the point at a particular time. This is shown for the second point in Figure 2.13.

If we take the coordinates where the tangent line crosses the y-axis and the $y = 50$ m line for the rise over the run, we find that $\Delta y = 30$ m and $\Delta t = 3$ s, so the slope is $m = \dfrac{\Delta y}{\Delta t} = \dfrac{30 \text{ m}}{3 \text{ s}} = 10 \dfrac{\text{m}}{\text{s}}$. You can find the slopes at the other times by drawing in the tangent lines at those points. You should find that the values in m/s from 1 s through 5 s are 20, 10, 0, −10, and −20.

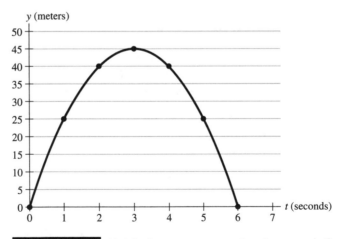

FIGURE 2.12 Height in meters versus time in seconds for an object thrown straight up with an initial velocity of $30 \dfrac{\text{m}}{\text{s}}$. The value of the acceleration due to gravity has been rounded to $10 \dfrac{\text{m}}{\text{s}^2}$.

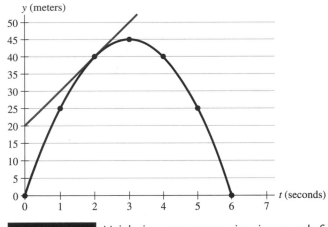

FIGURE 2.13   Height in meters versus time in seconds for an object thrown straight up with an initial velocity of $30\ \dfrac{m}{s}$, with a line drawn tangent to the point (2m, 40s) on the graph.

We now can find the slope of a line by taking the rise over the run. For a curve, we draw a straight line tangent to the curve at the point where we want to know the slope, and take the rise over the run for that tangent line. We can find the area under a straight line by using the coordinate values and the areas of triangles and rectangles. We won't usually need the area under a curve in an introductory course. ■

PRACTICE

1. Figure 2.14 shows a circle with its center at the origin. What is the slope of the lines tangent to the circle at the following points?

   a) (4,0)   b) (0, 4)   c) (–4, 0)   d) (0, –4)

2. Figure 2.15 shows a possible velocity versus time curve for a car. What is the slope when t varies from

   a) 0 s to 2 s?

   b) 2 s to 4 s?

   c) 4 s to 8 s?

   d) 8s to 10 s?

   e) 10 s to 12 s?

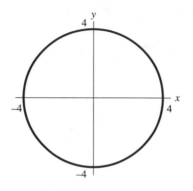

FIGURE 2.14 A circle with the x- and y-coordinates of the points where the circle crosses the axes shown.

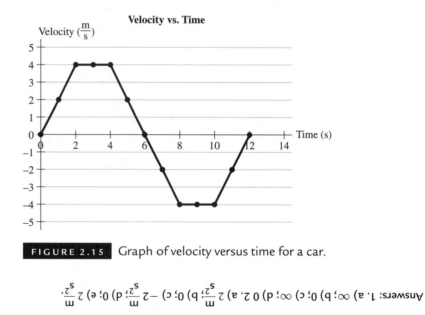

FIGURE 2.15 Graph of velocity versus time for a car.

Answers: 1. a) ∞; b) 0; c) ∞; d) 0 2. a) 0 2. a) 0 2 $\frac{m}{s^2}$; b) 0; c) $-2\frac{m}{s^2}$; d) $-2\frac{m}{s^2}$; e) 0; e) 2 $\frac{m}{s^2}$.

Trigonometry

If you will be taking physics for a health science or other major that does not require calculus, the right angle trigonometry presented here is all you will need. If you are taking physics for an engineering or science major that requires calculus, your calculus courses will review most other trigonometry you might need besides that presented here.

Therefore, we will review only the trigonometric relations that are used frequently, and a few other relationships you will need.

A trigonometric ratio is defined by the ratio of two sides of a right triangle. (One of the angles of a right triangle is 90°.) There are six such ratios: sine, cosine, tangent, secant, cosecant, and cotangent. Greek letters, such as θ (theta) and ϕ (phi)—pronounced thay-tuh and fie, respectively—are used to represent angles, figures formed by two intersecting sides. In any right triangle, there are two sides that form the right angle, and the hypotenuse, the side opposite to the right, or 90°, angle. Opposite means the side that is not one of the two sides forming the angle. Of the two sides forming an angle other than the 90° angle, the adjacent is the side other than the hypotenuse. See Figure 2.16.

✔ **QUICK CHECK**

Given the right triangle here, what are

1. $\sin \theta$?

2. $\cos \theta$?

3. $\tan \theta$?

Answers: 1. $\dfrac{b}{c}$, 2. $\dfrac{a}{c}$, 3. $\dfrac{b}{a}$.

Use the following shorthand: OPP = opposite, ADJ = adjacent, and HYP = hypotenuse. Then we define

$$\sin \theta = \frac{\text{OPP}}{\text{HYP}} \text{ (sine)};$$

$$\cos \theta = \frac{\text{ADJ}}{\text{HYP}} \text{ (cosine)};$$

$$\tan \theta = \frac{\text{OPP}}{\text{ADJ}} \text{ (tangent)}.$$

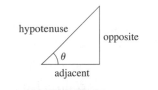

FIGURE 2.16   The sides of a right triangle in reference to the angle θ.

A mnemonic (memory device) to help with these is SOHCAHTOA for sin = opp/hyp; cos = adj/hyp; tan = opp/adj.

Used much less often but sometimes needed are

$$\operatorname{cosec} \theta = \frac{\text{HYP}}{\text{OPP}} = \frac{1}{\sin \theta} \text{ (cosecant)};$$

$$\sec \theta = \frac{\text{HYP}}{\text{ADJ}} = \frac{1}{\cos \theta} \text{ (secant)};$$

$$\operatorname{cotan} \theta = \frac{\text{ADJ}}{\text{OPP}} = \frac{1}{\tan \theta} \text{ (cotangent)}.$$

✔ QUICK CHECK

Use the definitions just given to find the sine, cosine, and tangent of angle ϕ in the triangle in the previous Quick Check.

Answers: 1. $\frac{c}{a}$; 2. $\frac{b}{c}$; 3. $\frac{b}{a}$.

TIME TO TRY

Given the right triangle shown, find the following:

1. $\sin \theta$

2. $\cos \theta$

3. $\tan \theta$

4. $\sin \phi$

5. $\cos \phi$

6. $\cot \phi$

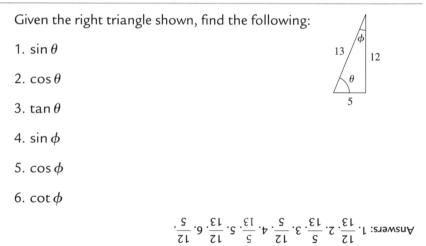

Answers: 1. $\frac{12}{13}$; 2. $\frac{5}{13}$; 3. $\frac{12}{5}$; 4. $\frac{5}{13}$; 5. $\frac{12}{13}$; 6. $\frac{12}{5}$.

The functions defined previously and their inverses—the angles found from the value of the trig functions, which we review in the Using Calculators for Finding Trig Functions section—cover most uses of trigonometry in the first physics course. However, you will also benefit from being familiar with some relations between trigonometric functions.

FIGURE 2.17   A standard right triangle.

TRIGONOMETRIC IDENTITIES

In this section, we look at the basic trig identities. There are many more than those given here, but these should cover almost any problem that might arise in an introductory physics course. The first one is based on Pythagoras's theorem: For the triangle shown in Figure 2.17, $a^2 + b^2 = c^2$.   Therefore, $1 = \dfrac{a^2}{c^2} + \dfrac{b^2}{c^2} = \left(\dfrac{a}{c}\right)^2 + \left(\dfrac{b}{c}\right)^2 = \sin^2\theta + \cos^2\theta$.

Note the distinction between $\sin 2\theta = \sin(2\theta)$ and $\sin^2\theta = (\sin\theta) \times (\sin\theta)$. You should also be aware that we can prove

$$\sin(A \pm B) = \sin A \cos B \pm \cos A \sin B \text{ and}$$
$$\cos(A \pm B) = \cos A \cos B \mp \sin A \sin B$$

for any two angles A and B, not necessarily those in a right triangle.

You will encounter $2\sin\theta\cos\theta = \sin\theta\cos\theta + \cos\theta\sin\theta = \sin(2\theta)$ when studying projectile motion.

For completeness, let a, b, and c be sides in any triangle, not necessarily a right triangle, and let A, B, and C be the angles opposite to those sides. Then the law of cosines is $c^2 = a^2 + b^2 - 2ab\cos C$, with equivalent equations for sides a or b, and the law of sines is $\dfrac{\sin A}{a} = \dfrac{\sin B}{b} = \dfrac{\sin C}{c}$.

WORKED EXAMPLE 2.8

1. One side of a right triangle is 6.0 m (meter) and the angle opposite to that side is 30°. Find the length of the hypotenuse, the other acute angle in the right triangle, and the length of the third side.

Answer: See the right triangle shown here.

Because $\sin(30°) = \dfrac{\text{OPP}}{\text{HYP}} = \dfrac{6.0 \text{ m}}{h}$,

$h = 6.0 \text{ m} \times \sin(30°) = 3.0 \text{ m}.$

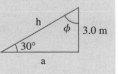

Because $\cos \phi = \dfrac{\text{ADJ}}{\text{HYP}} = \dfrac{3.0 \text{ m}}{6.0 \text{ m}} = 0.5$, $\phi = 60°$. (See the following Using Calculators for Finding Trig Functions section.) You could also have noticed that if one angle is 90° and the second one is 30°, the third angle must be 60° because the sum of the angles in a triangle is 180°. Finally, we can use Pythagoras's Theorem to find the third side, but let's practice using trig functions. Because $\cos 30° = \dfrac{\text{ADJ}}{\text{HYP}} = \dfrac{a}{6.0 \text{ m}}$, we can use a calculator to find that $a = 5.2$ m. Check this by using Pythagoras's theorem.

2. The law of refraction of light at a boundary between two different substances, such as air and glass, states that $n_1 \sin \theta_1 = n_2 \sin \theta_2$, where n_1 and n_2 are the indices of refraction of the first substance and the second substance, respectively, that light passes through; θ_1 is the angle between the light ray in the first substance and the line perpendicular to the boundary between the two substances; and θ_2 is the angle the light ray in the second substance makes with the same perpendicular line. See Figure 2.18.

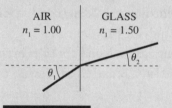

AIR
$n_1 = 1.00$

GLASS
$n_1 = 1.50$

FIGURE 2.18   The refraction of light as it passes from air into glass.

If $\theta_1 = 45°$, find θ_2.

Answer: We solve $n_1 \sin \theta_1 = n_2 \sin \theta_2$ for $\sin\theta_2$, and then use a calculator to find θ_2.

$$\sin \theta_2 = \frac{n_1}{n_2} \sin \theta_1 = \frac{1.00}{1.50} \sin 45° = \frac{0.707}{1.50} = 0.4714.$$

We keep an extra significant figure in our solution than within our equation because trig functions vary rapidly with angle. To determine θ_2, we need to find the inverse sine of 0.4714 or $\sin^{-1}(0.4714)$. If you press the second function key and then the sine key on your standard scientific calculator, you will find that $\theta_2 = 28.1°$ to three significant figures.

What was found here was an inverse to the sine of the angle. The sine of the angle is the function. The inverse sine, the inverse of the function, is the angle. In the next section, you will practice finding inverse trig functions.

USING CALCULATORS FOR FINDING TRIG FUNCTIONS AND INVERSE TRIG FUNCTIONS

TRIG FUNCTIONS To find $\sin \theta$, $\cos \theta$, and $\tan \theta$, be sure that your calculator is set for degrees, enter the value of the angle, and press the appropriate key. To find the other three trig functions, use

$$\operatorname{cosec} \theta = \frac{1}{\sin \theta}; \sec \theta = \frac{1}{\cos \theta}; \text{ and } \cot \theta = \frac{1}{\tan \theta}.$$

✔ **QUICK CHECK**

Find the sine, cosine, tangent, secant, cosecant, and cotangent of 22.5°.

Answer: sine 22.5° = 0.383; cosine 22.5° = 0.924; tangent 22.5° = 0.414; secant 22.5° = 1.082; cosecant 22.5° = 2.61, cotangent 22.5° = 2.41.

INVERSE TRIG FUNCTIONS Difficulties arise in going from the value of the trig function back to the angle, because trig functions are multiple-valued; more than one angle results in the same value of the function. Therefore, additional information is needed when finding an inverse. For example, $\sin 60° = \sin 120° = 0.8660$ and $\cos 60° = \cos(-60°) = 0.5000$. Given $0.8660 = \sin \theta$ and asked to find the angle, we need to know the quadrant the angle is in to determine the answer. Otherwise there are two possibilities. The quadrants are shown in Figure 2.19 in a plane defined by the x and y axes.

The best way to understand this is to try some examples.

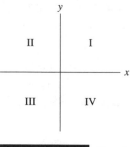

FIGURE 2.19   Quadrant positions of angles associated with trig functions.

TIME TO TRY

1. Given $\sin \theta = 0.8000$, find the possible angles θ.

2. Given $\sin \theta = -0.5000$, find the possible angles θ.

3. Given $\tan \theta = 1.0000$, find the possible angles θ.

Answers: 1. $\theta = 53.1°$ or $\theta = 180° - 53.1° = 126.9°$. **2.** $\theta = -30.0°$ or
$\theta = 180.0° + 30.0° = 210.0°$. Note that $-30.0°$ is the same as $+330.0°$.
3. $\theta = 45.0°$ or $\theta = 180.0° + 45.0° = 235°$.

Sketch these angles in the *x-y* plane to see why this is the case. Look up
http://www.mathwizz.com/algebra/help/help29.htm or an equivalent
site on the Web for more information on quadrants and the values of
trig functions.

VECTORS AND VECTOR COMPONENTS

The quantities you will use in pictorial, diagrammatic, and mathematical
representations of physical interactions will have directions as well as
magnitudes. A quantity with a magnitude and a direction is called a vector. Changes in position, called displacements, forces, velocities, electric
fields, and many others all have both direction and magnitude. First, you
will work with vectors relative to coordinate axes. Then the following
section will show how to calculate the projections of vectors on coordinate axes, these projections being the components of the vectors.

Any vector, such as displacement, may be drawn as a directed line or
arrow. Place the coordinate origin at the *tail* of the arrow and draw in *x*
and *y* axes, as in Figure 2.20.

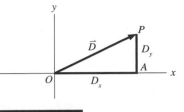

FIGURE 2.20   The scalar components of a vector.

The displacement, $\overrightarrow{D}$, is shown as a directed line. In addition, the line AP is drawn perpendicular to the *x*-axis. The segment of the positive *x*-axis cut off by the line AP is OA. OA, labeled D_x, is the projection of $\overrightarrow{D}$ on the *x*-axis. D_x is called the *x*-component of the vector $\overrightarrow{D}$.

Drop a perpendicular line from the head of $\overrightarrow{D}$ to the *y*-axis. Label the point where it cuts the *y*-axis point B. How does the length OB compare to the length AP?

The length OB is equal to AP. AP is labeled D_y. OB, or AP, is called the *y*-component of the vector $\overrightarrow{D}$. D_x and D_y are *scalar* components because they do not have arrows attached.

In Figure 2.21, OA and AP are vectors. They are called vector components of $\overrightarrow{D}$ because they have directions. They are the vectors $\overrightarrow{D}_x$ and $\overrightarrow{D}_y$.

Walk from O to A and then from A to P. You have undergone two displacements, $\overrightarrow{D}_x$ and $\overrightarrow{D}_y$, and have ended up at P. If you start at O and walk directly to P, the single displacement $\overrightarrow{D}$ will get you there. $\overrightarrow{D}$ is equivalent to the instruction "displacement $\overrightarrow{D}_x$ followed by displacement $\overrightarrow{D}_y$." Therefore,

$$\overrightarrow{D} = \overrightarrow{D}_x + \overrightarrow{D}_y.$$

Any vector is equal to the sum of its vector components along the *x*- and *y*-axes. ■

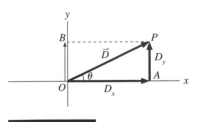

FIGURE 2.21   The vector components of a vector.

WORKED EXAMPLE 2.9

1. Suppose the magnitude of $\vec{D}_x$ is 3 m, and the magnitude of $\vec{D}_y$ is 4 m. Find the magnitude of $\vec{D}$.

   We find D from the Pythagorean theorem.
   $D^2 = D_x^2 + D_y^2 = (3\text{ m})^2 + (4\text{ m})^2 = (5\text{ m})^2$ so $D = 5$ m.

2. Suppose the magnitude of $\vec{D}$ is 10 m, and it is 53.1° counterclockwise from the x-axis. Find D_x and D_y.

   For this vector, $D_x = (10\text{ m})\cos 53.1° = (10\text{ m})(.8) = 8$ m and $D_y = (10\text{ m})\sin 53.1° = (10\text{ m})(.6) = 6$ m.

3. Given the magnitudes of $\vec{D}_x$ and $\vec{D}_y$, find $\vec{D}$. Given $\vec{D}$, find the magnitudes of $\vec{D}_x$ and $\vec{D}_y$.

   We use the same process we used before, but now in symbols: $D^2 = D_x^2 + D_y^2$. To find D_x and D_y, we use $D_x = D\cos\theta$ and $D_y = D\sin\theta$.

   To see this, look at Figure 2.21, in which $\sin\theta = \dfrac{D_y}{D}$ and $\cos\theta = \dfrac{D_x}{D}$. Thus, $D_x = D\cos\theta$, $D_y = D\sin\theta$. If you know D and θ, you know D_x and D_y. If you divide $D_y = D\sin\theta$ by $D_x = D\cos\theta$ you get $\tan\theta = \dfrac{D_y}{D_x}$. In addition, Pythagoras's theorem gives $D_x^2 + D_y^2 = D^2$. If you know D_x and D_y, you know D and θ. These equations are summarized here:

$$D_x = D\cos\theta$$

$$D_y = D\sin\theta$$

$$\tan\theta = \frac{D_y}{D_x}$$

$$D^2 = D_x^2 + D_y^2.$$

These equations hold for vectors in any quadrant as long as θ is always measured counterclockwise from the positive x-axis. Always measure θ consistently from the x-axis. That way you'll always get correct values for D_x and D_y from your calculator.

TIME TO TRY

Find the *x*- and *y*-components of the following vectors:

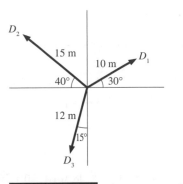

FIGURE 2.22   Three vectors in the *xy*-plane.

Answers: $D_{1x} = 10.0$ m cos $(30°) = 8.66$ m, $D_{1y} = 10.0$ m sin $(30°) = 5.0$ m,
$D_{2x} = 15.0$ m cos $(140°) = -11.5$ m, $D_{2y} = 15.0$ m sin $(140°) = 9.64$ m,
$D_{3x} = 12.0$ m cos $(255°) = -3.11$ m, $D_{3y} = 12.0$ m sin $(255°) = -11.6$ m

If you ride your bicycle to a class and then over to the cafeteria, we need to add the two displacements to get your net displacement. That means adding vectors. We do it by placing the tail of the second vector at the head of the first vector, as in Figure 2.23. It's like dogs sniffing: the head of the first dog at the second dog's tail.

What happens if you walk backward? You change direction. The negative of a vector has the same length but the opposite direction. We subtract vector 2 from vector 1 by adding the negative of vector 2 to vector 1 as in Figure 2.24.

To find the length of vectors added or subtracted in this way requires a ruler and a protractor, and is not accurate. It turns out that you can add vectors by adding their components. We can subtract vectors by

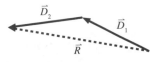

FIGURE 2.23   The dashed arrow shows the sum of the other two displacements.

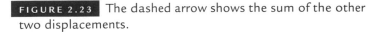

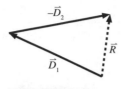

FIGURE 2.24 The result of subtracting vector 2 from vector 1.

subtracting components. You will use the resultant components to find the vector as in the previous examples.

Exponents, Logarithms, and Exponentials

If you know that 2 "squared" is four and that 3 "squared" is 9, you already know the most basic rule of exponents. "Square" is an instruction, written as the superscript 2, to multiply a quantity by itself. Thus, $2^2 = 4$ and $3^2 = 9$. In short, an exponent p is an instruction to multiply a number a or a symbol such as x by itself p times. If $a = 2$ and $p = 4$, $a^p = 2^4 = 2 \times 2 \times 2 \times 2 = 16$.

What is 2^6?

Answer:

$$2^6 = \underbrace{2 \times 2 \times 2 \times 2 \times 2 \times 2}_{6 \text{ times}} = 4 \times 4 \times 4 = 8 \times 8 = 64$$

LAWS OF EXPONENTS

A number of laws follow from this basic definition of exponents.

Law of Exponents I. $a^p \times a^q = a^{p+q}$, because

$$\underbrace{(a \times a \times a...a)}_{p \text{ times}} \times \underbrace{(a \times a \times a...a)}_{q \text{ times}} = \underbrace{(a \times a \times a...a)}_{p + q \text{ times}}.$$

Law of Exponents II. $\dfrac{a^p}{a^q} = a^{p-q}$ because $\dfrac{\underbrace{(a \times a \times a...a)}_{p \text{ times}}}{\underbrace{(a \times a \times a...a)}_{q \text{ times}}} =$

$\underbrace{(a \times a \times a...a)}_{p - q \text{ times}}$ owing to the q cancellations.

This assumes $p > q$.

From these we can deduce that $a^{-n} = \dfrac{1}{a^n}$, and $a^0 = 1$.

✔ **QUICK CHECK**

1. Show that $a^0 = 1$. (Hint: Use Law II.)
2. Show that $a^{\frac{1}{2}} = \sqrt{a}$. (Hint: Use Law I.)
3. What is $2^{2.5}$?
4. What is 2^{-4}?

Answers: 1. Because $\dfrac{a^n}{a^n} = a^{n-n} = a^0$, $a^0 = 1$. 2. Because $a^{\frac{1}{2}} \times a^{\frac{1}{2}} = a^1 = a$ and $\sqrt{a} \times \sqrt{a} = a$, we find that $a^{\frac{1}{2}} = \sqrt{a}$. 3. This is $2^{2.5} = 2 \times 2 \times \sqrt{2} = 4 \times 1.414 = 5.657$. 4. Because $2^{-4} = \dfrac{1}{2^4}$, $2^{-4} = \dfrac{1}{16}$.

TIME TO TRY

1. What are $9^{\frac{1}{2}}$ and 9^0?
2. Show that $a^{-n} = \dfrac{1}{a^n}$. (Law of Exponents III)
3. Prove $(a^n)^p = a^{p \times n}$. (Law of Exponents IV)
4. Prove: When $a^r = p$, then $a = \sqrt[r]{p} = p^{\frac{1}{r}}$. (Law of Exponents V)

If $p = 0$, then

$$a^{0-n} = a^{-n} = \frac{\overbrace{(a \times a \times a \cdots a)}^{0\ \text{times}}}{\underbrace{(a \times a \times a \cdots a)}_{n\ \text{times}}}.$$

Answers: 1. ∓ 3 and 1. 2. If $p > q$, then

$$\frac{\overbrace{(a \times a \times a \cdots a)}^{p\ \text{times}}}{\underbrace{(a \times a \times a \cdots a)}_{q\ \text{times}}} = \frac{\overbrace{(a \times a \times a \cdots a)}^{p-q\ \text{times}}}{1}.$$

$$\overbrace{(a \times a \times a \cdots a)}^{0\ times}$$

But $\dfrac{\overbrace{(a \times a \cdots a)}^{n\ times}}{\overbrace{(a \times a \cdots a)}^{0\ times}} = \dfrac{\overbrace{(a \times a \cdots a)}^{n-0\ times}}{1} = \dfrac{\overbrace{(a \times a \cdots a)}^{n\ times}}{1} = \dfrac{1}{a^{-n}}.$ Therefore,

$a^{-n} = \dfrac{1}{a^n}.$ 3. We use our basic definition: $(a^n)^p =$

$$a^{nx} = \overbrace{\underbrace{(a \times a \times a \cdots a)}_{n\ times} \times \underbrace{(a \times a \times a \cdots a)}_{n\ times} \times \underbrace{(a \times a \times a \cdots a)}_{n\ times} \times \cdots}^{p\ times}$$

4. Given $a^r = p$, then by 3, $(a^r)^{\frac{1}{r}} = a^{\frac{r}{r}} = a^1 = a = p^{\frac{1}{r}}.$ Therefore,

$\overbrace{(a \times a \cdots a)}^{r\ times} = p.$ But the quantity that equals p when multiplied by itself

r times is $\sqrt[r]{p}.$ Thus, $a = \sqrt[r]{p} = p^{\frac{1}{r}}.$

ADDITIONAL RULES FOR EXPONENTS A few additional rules follow directly from the preceding rules:

Law of Exponents VI. $\sqrt[n]{a} \times \sqrt[n]{b} = \sqrt[n]{ab}.$

Law of Exponents VII. $\dfrac{\sqrt[n]{a}}{\sqrt[n]{b}} = \sqrt[n]{\dfrac{a}{b}}.$

Law of Exponents VIII. $\sqrt[m]{\sqrt[n]{a}} = \sqrt[m \times n]{a}.$

✔ **QUICK CHECK**

1. Find $\sqrt[6]{64}$ without the use of a calculator.

2. Simplify $\sqrt[5]{\dfrac{32}{x^3}}.$

Answers: 1. $\sqrt[6]{64} = \sqrt[3 \times 2]{64} = \sqrt[3]{\sqrt[2]{64}} = \sqrt[3]{8} = 2.$
2. $2 \times x^{-\frac{3}{5}}.$

EXPONENTIALS

We frequently encounter situations where something doubles or decreases by half in a given time interval. Examples are bacterial growth in a medium, or nuclear decay. Although human population growth is also exponential, its rate of increase decreases as a country becomes more prosperous.

A standard example of an exponential change is given in the story of the philosopher who specified his reward as follows. He was to receive one grain of rice the first day, two grains the second day, four the third day, eight the fourth day, and so on through thirty days. The number $1 + 2 + 4 + 8 + 16 + 32 + 64 + 128 + 256 + ...$ seems fairly innocuous, but on the thirtieth day the number $2^{29} = 536,870,000$ would involve major transport problems.

As you can see, this doubling or halving involves 2^n. For some purposes it is more convenient to use 10^n because 10 is the basis of our number system and also is larger than 2. The standard way of writing numbers in scientific notation is as 2.738×10^4 rather than as 27,380, where 4 represents the number of places that the decimal is moved to the right when the number is written without scientific notation. We dealt with why we want to avoid that last zero in an earlier section.

The other base used frequently in physics is e. Expressions of the form e^{at} or e^{-at} occur often. Your calculator has an e^x key. Usually, you enter a number, press the second function key and then the e^x.

✔ **QUICK CHECK**

Use your calculator to find the values of $e^{-2.1}$ and $e^{+2.1}$.

Answer: $e^{-2.1} = 0.122$ and $e^{+2.1} = 8.17$.

EXPONENTIAL DECAY AND GROWTH We can look at exponential growth and decay in several different ways. If you start with N_0 pairs of rabbits, and the rabbits double n times, you end up with $N = N_0(2)^n$ rabbits. But if the rabbits increase by a fraction b, for example 0.4, in a month, then n equals b multiplied by the number of months. Thus we can write $N = N_0(2)^{bt}$. We can also look at the amount $\Delta N = N - N_0$ by which the number of rabbits changes in a given time. Because the increase in the number of pairs of rabbits must depend on the number of pairs we started with—this is an example of ratio and proportion—we must also have $\Delta N = cN_0$, where c is a constant. This equation can be shown to have a solution $N = N_0 e^{at}$. Setting our two solutions equal we see that we can use any base. Here $2^{bt} = e^{at}$ and $at \ln e = bt \ln 2$, so $b = a \dfrac{\ln e}{\ln 2}$. It is most common to use the base e, and we'll do that from now on. See the following section on logarithms for more about e.

When a quantity doubles or halves in equal time intervals, that is the same as exponential growth or decay. To find the value of N at time t, multiply N_0 by 2 or $\dfrac{1}{2}$ n times, that is, the number $n = bt$ times, where n does not have to be an integer, because t can be any time; or multiply N_0 by e^{at} where a is a positive or negative constant. Both a and b, which have units $\dfrac{1}{\text{time unit}}$, are called time constants. ■

✔ **QUICK CHECK**

1. If $a = \dfrac{3.5}{y}$, how long does it take for N to double?

2. If $a = -\dfrac{3.5}{y}$, how long does it take for n to decrease by one-half?

Answers: 1. $\dfrac{N}{N_0} = e^{at} = 2$. Therefore, $\ln (e^{at}) = at = \ln 2$. (Remember that the logarithm is the exponent to which the base is raised.) Thus,

$t = \dfrac{\ln 2}{a} = \dfrac{0.693}{\dfrac{3.5}{y}} = 0.198 \ y$. 2. $\dfrac{N}{N_0} = \dfrac{1}{2} = e^{-at}$. Therefore,

$\ln (e^{-at}) = -at = \ln \left(\dfrac{1}{2}\right) = \ln 1 - \ln 2 = -\ln 2$ and $t = \dfrac{0.693}{\dfrac{3.5}{y}} = 0.198 \ y$.

The decay products may themselves decay. Then, given the value of a for the decay product, you repeat the same type of calculation. Only a few topics in the introductory physics course use exponentials or logarithms—intensity levels, eye and ear responses, nuclear decay, complex representations of alternating currents, and other uses of phasors—but you need to understand exponentials and logarithms thoroughly when those topics arise. (Phasors are a type of exponential.)

LOGARITHMS

A logarithm is an exponent. If $a^x = N$, then the logarithm to the base a of N is x. This is written as $\log_a N = x$. That's all there is to it: The logarithm is the power to which the base is raised to give the number.

Let's start with the base 10.

If $10^3 = 1000$, what is the log of 1,000 to the base 10?

Answer: 3

What is the log of 595 to the base 10?

Answer: It is a number x such that $10^x = 595$. Before calculators were available, people used tables to find these logarithms. Now we enter 595 in our calculators, press the "2nd function" and "log" keys, and find that the answer is 2.7745. Thus, $\log_{10}(595) = 2.7745$.

✔ **QUICK CHECK**

Find the log to the base 10 of 0.25.

Answer: $\log_{10}(0.25) = -0.602$, so $10^{-0.602} = 0.25$

One special number occurs frequently not only in math, but also in physical processes such as exponential growth and decay. It is called "e," where $e = 2.7187818$ to eight figures. When logarithms have the base e, they are called natural logarithms. The base e occurs in calculus where it occurs as an important limit and crops up frequently. Note that your calculator has an "ln" key as well as a "log" key; the ln key represents natural logs. Find it now, and use it to solve the following example.

What is $\ln_e(1000)$?

Enter 1,000 in your calculator, press the second function key, and then press the ln key. You should find that $\ln_e(1000) = 6.9078$ to five figures.

RULES OF LOGARITHMS Because logs to the base 10 or lns to the base e or logs to any base are exponents, the rules of logarithms follow from the rules of exponents.

Rule of Logarithms I. $\log(MN) = \log M + \log N$

$\ln(ab) = \ln a + \ln b$

Rule of Logarithms II. $\log\left(\dfrac{M}{N}\right) = \log M - \log N$

$\ln\left(\dfrac{a}{b}\right) = \ln a - \ln b$

Rule of Logarithms III. $\log(M^n) = n \log M$ $\ln(a^n) = n \ln a$

Rule of Logarithms IV. $\log \sqrt[r]{M} = \dfrac{\log M}{r}$ $\ln \sqrt[r]{a} = \dfrac{\ln a}{r}$

PRACTICE

1. Find log and ln of a) 18.0; b) 0.0018.

2. Find log and ln of a) 5^9; b) $\sqrt[3]{15}$.

3. Find log and ln of a) $x^2 y^3 z$; b) $\sqrt[3]{u}\ \sqrt{w}$.

Answers: 1. a) 1.255 and 2.890; b) −2.745 and −6.320. **2. a)** 9 × log 5 = 6.290 and 9 × ln 5 = 14.48; b) log 15 = $\frac{1}{3}$ log $(15\frac{1}{3})$ = 0.392 and 0.903. **3. a)** 2 log x + 3 log y + log z and 2 ln x + 3 ln y + ln z **b)** log $(u^{\frac{1}{3}}w^{\frac{1}{2}})$ = $\frac{3}{1}$ log u + $\frac{5}{1}$ log w and ln $(u^{\frac{1}{3}}w^{\frac{1}{2}})$ = $\frac{3}{1}$ ln u + $\frac{5}{1}$ ln w.

Many physical systems are logarithmic. It takes 10 violinists to sound twice as loud as one violinist because the sense of loudness is logarithmic. Thus the standard unit of loudness, the decibel, is proportional to the logarithm to the base 10 of the intensity of a sound.

INVERSE LOGARITHMS

Just as you can find an angle when given its sine or cosine, you can find a number when given its log or ln. It's much easier than finding inverse trig functions because logarithms are single-valued: There is only one number that corresponds to a given value of a log or ln.

WORKED EXAMPLE 2.10

Given that $\log_{10} N = 3.20$ and that $\ln_e M = 3.20$, find $N + M$. It should be clear that this problem asks us to find two separate quantities, N and M, and add them.

To find N, enter 3.20 in your calculator. Then press the second function and the 10^x key for the anti log.

WHY?

Because the logarithm is the exponent to which the base is raised to give the number, the logarithm is the exponent that goes with the base 10. Pick the correct base and you have the number.

To find M, enter 3.20 in your calculator, then press the second function key and the e^x key. The result is M.

Thus, $10^{3.2} = 1585$ and $e^{3.20} = 24.5$, so $N + M = 1610$, where we have rounded the result to four significant figures. (Check these calculations on your calculator.)

PRACTICE

1. Given $\log_{10} N = -2.22$, find N.

2. Given $\ln_e M = 6.666$, find M.

Answers: 1. 1.603×10^{-3}, 2. 785.2

Transferring Knowledge to New Contexts

If you live in a city with more than one bus line, you know that you can reach your destination by asking for a transfer when you pay your fare. The transfer is a piece of paper that lists the bus line you are on, the bus lines to which you can transfer, and the date and time when you paid your fare. You can then exit the bus and transfer to the connecting bus without paying a second fare.

It would be great if we could take what we learned in math courses and apply it all directly to physics courses, transferring the knowledge as we transfer buses. Unfortunately, a large body of research shows that what we learned in math is tied to the symbols that were used in math, and is even associated with the locations where we used that information. Cues from our surroundings, teachers, and fellow students, and from our activities at the time, make it easier to access knowledge that was learned in the same surroundings with the same teachers, students, class exercises, and homework.

For that reason, some Quick Check and Time to Try problems in this chapter have used symbols for physical quantities rather than just the x and y symbols used in math classes. In this section, we will practice solving math we have already used, but with different symbols or with physical units attached. Rather than simply 3, it will be 3 m for 3 meters or 3 μF for 3 microfarads.

Keep in mind that we learn math at three levels. The first level is numbers. Numbers give us a concrete realization of groups of objects. The number 5 is common to five birds, five fingers, five trees, etc. In the next step we use a symbol for a number: x or N or I or whatever symbol we choose can stand for any number that gives it a value for a particular system or object or problem. At the third level, a symbol can stand for another symbol.

An example of symbols standing for symbols, as mentioned earlier, is the equation for a straight line: $y = mx + b$. If we know how to work with this equation we also know how to solve $v = v_0 + at$, where velocity depends on the initial velocity, the acceleration, and the time. We know how to solve $V = V_0 - Ex$ for the potential at a point x when the potential at the origin is V_0 and an electric field E points in the positive x-axis direction. If you start to realize consciously that what you learned in math is a summary in symbols of what you need to use in physics, it will become easier to apply that knowledge to physics. But only practice will accomplish the goal.

Here are some practice exercises applying math that you know—common denominators and complex fractions—to typical physics measures:

TIME TO TRY

1. Given $\dfrac{1}{4\ \mu F} - \dfrac{1}{5\ \mu F} = \dfrac{1}{C}$, find the capacitance C in μF (microfarads).

2. Given $\dfrac{4\,\Omega}{\dfrac{1}{2\,\mu F} + \dfrac{1}{3\,\mu F}}$ = _____ s, find the missing time constant.

(Here the Greek capital letter omega, Ω, stands for ohm, the unit of electrical resistance. A formula like this may arise when two capacitors and a resistor are in a series circuit.)

3. Simplify the left side of this equation for the time constant τ:

$\dfrac{R}{\dfrac{1}{C_1} + \dfrac{1}{C_2} + \dfrac{1}{C_3}} = \tau$. Here we have used the symbols for three

different capacitances and one resistance.

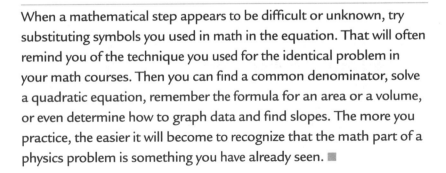

Answers: 1. We find a common denominator: $\dfrac{5}{20\,\mu F} - \dfrac{4}{20\,\mu F} = \dfrac{1}{20\,\mu F}$, so $C = 20\,\mu F$. 2. We first find a common denominator, and then use the rule for complex fractions:

$$\dfrac{4\,\Omega}{\dfrac{1}{2\,\mu F} + \dfrac{1}{3\,\mu F}} = \dfrac{4\,\Omega}{\dfrac{3}{6\,\mu F} + \dfrac{2}{6\,\mu F}} = \dfrac{4\,\Omega}{\dfrac{5}{6\,\mu F}} = 4\,\Omega \times \dfrac{6\,\mu F}{5} = \dfrac{24}{5}\,\mu F.$$

3. You should be able to show that

$$\tau = \dfrac{R}{\left[\dfrac{C_1 C_2 C_3}{C_2 C_3 + C_1 C_3 + C_1 C_2}\right]} = \dfrac{C_1 C_2 C_3}{C_2 C_3 + C_1 C_3 + C_1 C_2}\,R.$$ You have solved for

the time constant for three capacitors in series with a resistor.

When a mathematical step appears to be difficult or unknown, try substituting symbols you used in math in the equation. That will often remind you of the technique you used for the identical problem in your math courses. Then you can find a common denominator, solve a quadratic equation, remember the formula for an area or a volume, or even determine how to graph data and find slopes. The more you practice, the easier it will become to recognize that the math part of a physics problem is something you have already seen. ■

The examples in the Time to Try section have also illustrated the need for combining skills. In (2) and (3), you first had to find a common denominator and then simplify a complex fraction. The next chapter will show you that we first analyze observations through pictures and diagrams and reasoning before we come up with mathematical representations of the phenomena. Math is the last step in physics, not the first.

Final Stretch!

Now that you have finished reading this chapter it is time to stretch your brain and check how much you have learned.

WHAT DID YOU LEARN?

- How to estimate the results of calculations

- Rounding, significant figures, scientific notation, and standard prefixes

- Use of calculators for numerical and trigonometric operations

- The solution of simultaneous linear equations and of quadratic equations

- How to work with common denominators and complex fractions

- Use of proportional reasoning in direct, continued, and inverse proportions

- Graphing, including finding slopes of and areas under graphs

- Graphs of nonlinear relationships

- Trigonometric functions and identities

- The representation of physical quantities by vectors

- How to calculate vector components

- How to work with exponents, logarithms, and exponentials

- The need for conscious application to be able to transfer math knowledge to physics

WEB RESOURCES

For additional sources online, type in boldface section headings such as rounding, scientific notation, simultaneous equations, proportions, etc. into a search engine. If you use Google, a very general article at a high level will be listed first, but if you continue checking entries you will find one at a level just right for you. Sites like the Math League and Purplemath tend to offer easy examples.

> ■ *A site that you might not immediately think of, but that offers help with simultaneous equations is*
>
> **http://www.allaboutcircuits.com/vol_5/chpt_4/11.html**

Websites will provide many extra practice exercises. Note that sites at grade school, middle school, high school, and college level will all be listed in no particular order. You will probably want mostly high school level math reviews.

3 Physics Concepts, Part I

When you complete this chapter, you should be able to:

- Explain how to define and calculate the following:
    - Position
    - Displacement
    - Speed
    - Velocity
    - Change in velocity
    - Acceleration
    - Weight
    - Work
    - Kinetic energy
    - Gravitational potential energy
- State Newton's First, Second, and Third laws
- Draw work-energy bar charts

Introductions to the material of courses like biology or chemistry might start with terminology. In biology, you can learn the names of the different types of leaves and their different possible arrangements on a stem, such as opposite or alternating. Because physics started out describing everyday phenomena (things we see around us), it kept the same terminology used by people every day while changing the meanings in line with experimental discoveries. Although the technical meanings of the words as scientific terms changed, the words kept the same meanings in everyday speech. This means that anyone who studies physics has to learn a whole new set of meanings for words he or she already knows well. Trying to change our deep-set beliefs about what words mean is just as hard as trying to change political or religious beliefs when challenged by someone holding different views. In this chapter we won't need to discuss politics or religion, but we will emphasize concepts—as opposed to mere terminology—in everything we do.

Your Starting Point

Let's look at some terms and beliefs that can give you trouble. Although we have not yet provided exact definitions, see if you can decide whether the following sentences are true or false.

1. If you break out in a sweat when pushing on an immovable boulder, you are doing work.   T F

2. You may travel a distance of two miles but have a zero displacement.   T F

3. For an acceleration to occur, your car must increase in speed.   T F

4. A car stuck on railroad tracks gets demolished by the locomotive because the locomotive exerts a bigger force on the car than the car does on the locomotive.   T F

5. If John pushes on a car, it acquires an acceleration of $0.5 \frac{m}{s^2}$. If John's identical twin Edgar joins in and also pushes on that same car with a force of equal magnitude it may have an acceleration of $0 \frac{m}{s^2}$.   T F

6. Heat is energy stored at a high temperature.   T F

7. A ball stops rolling because it uses up the force that started it moving.   T F

8. You move forward when walking because your feet push you forward.   T F

9. Friction always slows objects down.   T F

10. An impulse is a large force.   T F

Answers: 1. False. The physics definition of work on an object combines a force on that object with a change of position of that object. If there is no change in position there is no work *on* the object. Weird? We'll see why this definition makes sense later on. 2. True. Displacement is the difference between the position at the end of a motion and the position at the beginning. If you drive to a friend's house and then return home, you are back where you started. There is no displacement, even if you traveled a distance of several miles each way. 3. False. A velocity has a direction and a magnitude in physics. Any change in a velocity is called an acceleration. Even if the magnitude, the speed, stays constant, a change in direction means that there is an acceleration. And a decrease as well as an increase in magnitude in velocity is also an acceleration. 4. False. Think about the following: a. You step on an ant. Which exerts the bigger force: your foot on the ant or the ant on your foot? b. Is it possible that your foot and the ant exert forces of equal magnitude on one another? We'll return to these questions later. 5. True. This involves scientific reasoning as well as internalized knowledge. How should Edgar push so that the force he exerts cancels the force John exerts? 6. False. Physicists themselves can be careless about the term "heat," but properly used, it refers only to thermal energy moving from one body to another because the two bodies have different temperatures. The thermal energy content of a body depends on the size and temperature of the body and that particular material's ability to store thermal energy. A ton of iron can store a lot more energy than the head of a pin. 7. False. Try rolling the same ball at the same initial speed on a very rough level surface, on a moderately rough level surface, and on a very smooth, possibly oiled level surface. What might the ball do on a surface with no roughness whatsoever? "Friction" is the word we use to describe "roughness"; you can feel friction by rubbing your hand lightly on a piece of sandpaper. 8. False. Suppose someone gave you a quick shove forward while you were standing at the edge of a cliff. What would you do in this life-and-death situation? Stand with your toes at the edge of a sheet of paper you have placed on the floor. Then have someone give you a moderate push when you are not expecting it. What do you do in order not to step on the paper, that is, not to go over the edge of the cliff? We'll discuss this answer later.

9. False. What makes objects move when they are dropped onto a conveyor belt? The conveyor belt exerts a force that is perpendicular to the surface of the object to stop its fall, but the conveyor belt also has to drag the object along. Otherwise the object would slip and stay in the same place. The conveyor belt has to exert a friction force parallel to the surface of the object to accelerate it so that it eventually moves at the same speed as the conveyor belt. What would happen if the conveyor belt were made of Teflon®, a slippery substance?

10. False. This is an example of a technical term having a very different meaning from the same word used in everyday language. An irresistible desire to purchase something you can't afford may be an impulse brought about by modern advertising. In physics, an impulse is the product of the force acting on an object times the length of time that the force acts on that object.

These questions and answers should have made clear to you that what you have to look out for in physics is clarity of ideas, not just math. You must know what each term means. In particular, you must know how to *measure* position, displacement, velocity, acceleration, force, momentum, work, energy, and anything else you want to use in calculations. The mental connection you make between the definition and the measurement procedure will help keep you from reverting to only that knowledge you possess before studying physics.

The part of physics that includes motion, both linear and rotational; forces and torques; energy and work; and momentum, linear and angular, is called mechanics. The study of motion, called *kinematics*, is the first topic we will address.

Kinematics

POSITION AND DISPLACEMENT

The ancient Greeks were pretty smart. They took geometric reasoning to a high level, knew the Earth was a sphere, and had advanced theories of drama and poetry, but they never got very far with the study of motion. They were able to do calculations with angular motion of the sun, moon, and known planets, but they never did the same thing for linear motions. A long time passed before these omissions were corrected. We are fortunate that these studies of motion have been carried out, and we can use the results.

Start with position. Your position is where you are right now: sitting at a desk or lying on a couch or on the floor. But how would you describe your position to me? And how would you assign a numerical value to it?

Describe in writing your position to me so that I can find you while you remain in that position. (Note that the ambiguous second "position" in the last sentence could also refer to how your limbs are arranged.)

You might have written, "Milky Way Galaxy, Planet Earth, Columbus, Ohio, USA, Tower Dorm, Room 1525, seated at my desk." Another student might have written the same thing but specified Room 1532.

I certainly could find both of you. But suppose I now ask you how far apart the two of you are. You have to get a measuring tape, a ruler, or a yardstick.

In physics we are always interested in how far apart two objects are, or how far one object has moved. In the dorm, the architect's plans specify the distances between the two rooms, whether or not the contractor followed the plans exactly. Because we'll look at motion in a straight line first, we need to specify positions along a line, which the mathematicians have already described for us.

WORKED EXAMPLE 3.1

How do we specify positions along a straight line in a math problem?

Answer: We use a coordinate axis. We draw a line that represents the actual physical space graphically. Let's say that we want to look at the motion of cars on a road. Highways usually have mile markers every tenth of a mile.

This is the actual physical situation we have in mind when we idealize the situation to a single line, the coordinate axis, and the cars to points.

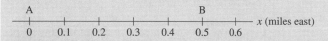

FIGURE 3.1 An idealized pictorial representation of a car at two different positions, A and B, on a highway with distances indicated in tenths of a mile.

Figure 3.1 represents the physical situation in an idealized form so that we can read the positions directly from the diagram. In physics, we'll always start with pictures and words, progress to diagrams, and then go on to graphs and equations. Now let's answer some questions based on Figure 3.1.

Suppose it takes the car 30 s ("s" is the standard abbreviation for second) to go from A to B while moving at constant speed. (Use your instinct about the concept of speed: We'll define it shortly.) How long did it take the car to go 0.1 mi? ("mi" is the standard symbol for mile.)

If it takes 30 s to travel 0.5 mi, the distance between A and B, then it takes 6 s to travel 0.1 mi. (Note that this is proportional reasoning.)

Suppose it takes 30 s for the car to go back from B to A. How long did it take the car to go 0.1 mi, 0.2 mi?

The return trip takes the same amount of time as the initial trip, so it covers 0.1 mi and 0.2 mi in 6 s and 12 s, respectively.

How do we distinguish between going from A to B and returning from B to A?

Answer: There is more than one way to specify this. We can state that we are heading east in going from A to B and west in heading from B to A. We can say that we first go 0.5 mi in the positive x-axis direction and then 0.5 mi in the negative x-axis direction. Either of these works, but we have to state the time as an additional piece of information.

Instinctively we know that longer distances take longer times to cover, which suggests that in distance problems we need to know a ratio of how far to how long an object has traveled. Therefore, we have the following definitions:

Distance. Imagine a roll of string is fixed at point A and the other end is tied to your car so that string unrolls as you drive, until you reach point B. Stretch the string out straight and measure its length: That result is the total distance you have traveled. (If you head back, imagine that the string goes around a stake at point B so it has to keep unwinding as you return.) Distance is always positive. Distance is the length measured by a ruler, yardstick, tape measure, laser, or any equivalent device when the string is straightened out.

Displacement. Displacement is the difference between a body's position at two different locations, as noted by coordinates. If the displacement is from one point to another on a coordinate axis, such as posts at two different mile markers, it can refer to the same time. If the displacement is of a body as it moves from the initial to the final position, such as a car moving from one mile marker to another, it represents the change in position over the time required for the movement. For motion on a straight line, displacement is what you read on the coordinate axis, still the x-axis, at the later time, x_f, minus what you read at the earlier time, x_i: $x_f - x_i$. We indicate relative changes by using Δ, the capital Greek letter delta, so $\Delta x = x_f - x_i$. When studying motion, Δ always refers to a value at a later time minus a value at an earlier time, but not necessarily to a greater value minus a lesser value.

There are instances where x_f has a smaller value than x_i. For example, let's say you started on the road at mile marker 5.6 mi and moved in the direction of decreasing mile marker distances, to post 2.3 mi. In this case, $x_i = 5.6$ mi and $x_f = 2.3$ mi.

TIME TO TRY

Jennie needs a new pair of jeans. She leaves home—point A in Figure 3.2—at time t_{A1} and drives due east to store B, arriving at time t_{B1} and leaving at time t_{B2}. She then drives to store C, arriving at time t_{C1}. She finds that store B has a lower price, so she leaves store C at time t_{C2} and arrives at store B at time t_{B3}. She leaves store B at time t_{B4} and arrives home at time t_{A2}.

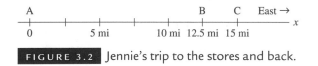

FIGURE 3.2 Jennie's trip to the stores and back.

1. What is the distance in miles to store B from home, point A?

2. What is the displacement of store B from home, point A?

3. What is the distance from store B to store C?

4. What is the displacement of store C from store B?

5. What is the distance to home from store B?

6. What is the displacement of home, point A, from store B?

Answers: 1. 12.5 mi. **2.** +12.5 mi. (We either have to say 12.5 miles to the right, or 12.5 mi east, or use the plus sign to give the direction of the displacement relative to the coordinate axis, directed east.) **3.** 2.5 mi. **4.** +2.5 mi (or 2.5 mi east). **5.** 12.5 mi. **6.** −12.5 mi (or 12.5 mi west).

SPEED AND VELOCITY

In any motion in life we are as much interested in how long it takes us to get there as in the distance we cover. If Jennie leaves home at 2:00 PM and wants to wear her new jeans when meeting her friend at 3:30 PM, she has to keep an eye on her wristwatch or cell phone. Let's assume she lives on a country road where there are no stoplights, so there are no extra time-consuming stops. Let's assume the times are t_{A1} = 2:00 PM; t_{B1} = 2:15 PM; t_{B2} = 2:23 PM; t_{C1} = 2:30 PM; t_{C2} = 2:38 PM; t_{B3} = 2:45 PM; t_{B4} = 2:55 PM; and t_{A2} = 3:08 PM.

We'll check out time intervals first. A time interval is a "length" of time, the later clock reading minus the earlier clock reading, again indicated by the capital Greek letter delta Δ: $\Delta t = t_f - t_i$.

✔ **QUICK CHECK**

What are the time intervals required for Jennie to go from

1. home to store B?

2. store B to store C?

3. store C back to store B?

4. store B back home?

Answer: 1. 15 min. **2.** 7 min. **3.** 7 min. **4.** 13 min.

Now we can calculate average speeds and average velocities. The **average speed** is the ratio of the distance traveled to the time taken, the time interval. The **average velocity** is the ratio of the displacement to the time taken, the time interval.

TIME TO TRY

1. What is Jennie's average speed when going from home to store B?

2. What is her average velocity when going from home to store B?

3. What is her average speed when going from store B to store C?

4. What is her average velocity when going from store B to store C?

5. What is her average speed when going from store C back to store B?

6. What is her average velocity when going from store C back to store B?

7. What is her average speed when going back home from store B?

8. What is her average velocity when going back home from store B?

Answers: 1. Jennie's average speed is the ratio of distance to time:
$$\frac{12.5 \text{ mi}}{15 \text{ min}} = 0.83 \frac{\text{mi}}{\text{min}}.$$ Note that this has no direction; it's just a number, a magnitude with units. 2. Jennie's average velocity is the ratio of displacement to time:
$$\frac{+12.5 \text{ mi}}{15 \text{ min}} = +0.83 \frac{\text{mi}}{\text{min}} = 0.83 \frac{\text{mi}}{\text{min}}, \text{ east.}$$ Note that this has a direction. For motion in a straight line, a + or − sign relative to the coordinate axis we have introduced is sufficient to indicate direction along that line, although we can provide the same information by stating the direction, such as east or west.

3. Her average speed is the ratio of distance to time: $$\frac{2.5 \text{ mi}}{7.0 \text{ min}} = 0.36 \frac{\text{mi}}{\text{min}}.$$

4. Her average velocity is the ratio of displacement to time:
$$\frac{+2.5 \text{ mi}}{7.0 \text{ min}} = +0.36 \frac{\text{mi}}{\text{min}} = 0.36 \frac{\text{mi}}{\text{min}}, \text{ east.}$$ 5. Her average speed is the ratio of distance to time: $$\frac{2.5 \text{ mi}}{7.0 \text{ min}} = 0.36 \frac{\text{mi}}{\text{min}}.$$ 6. Her average velocity is the ratio of displacement to time:
$$\frac{-2.5 \text{ mi}}{7.0 \text{ min}} = -0.36 \frac{\text{mi}}{\text{min}} = (+)0.36 \frac{\text{mi}}{\text{min}}, \text{ west.}$$

7. Her average speed is the ratio of distance to time: $$\frac{12.5 \text{ mi}}{13 \text{ min}} = 0.96 \frac{\text{mi}}{\text{min}}.$$

8. Her average velocity is the ratio of displacement to time:
$$\frac{-12.5 \text{ mi}}{13 \text{ min}} = -0.96 \frac{\text{mi}}{\text{min}} = (+)0.96 \frac{\text{mi}}{\text{min}}, \text{ west.}$$

If you understand the sign conventions in the preceding eight answers, you are in good shape to deal with graphical representations of motion as presented in Chapter 5.

CHANGE IN VELOCITY AND ACCELERATION

Travel on a highway would not be as dangerous as it is now if everyone drove at the same speed, and cars entered the highway only after having reached that speed. Even so, velocities, which have direction, would change every time there was a curve in the road. On a real highway, people travel at different speeds and different velocities. They veer out of their lanes while on cell phones or text-messaging. Because entering cars are moving at lower velocities than cars already on the road, their velocities clearly change as soon as they are on the highway. We'll look at changes in velocity first, and then at accelerations, the rates of change of velocities.

✔ **QUICK CHECK**

(Note our switch to metric units.)

1. At 2:19 AM, Cherie is driving west at 60 $\frac{m}{s}$. At 2:20 AM she is driving west at 40 $\frac{m}{s}$. What is Δv, the change in her velocity?

2. At 2:19 AM Joey is driving west at 60 $\frac{m}{s}$. At. 2:23 AM he is driving east at 40 $\frac{m}{s}$. What is Δv, the change in his velocity?

Answers: 1. Here $\Delta v = v_f - v_i = 40 \frac{m}{s}$, west $- 60 \frac{m}{s}$, west $= -20 \frac{m}{s}$, west $= +20 \frac{m}{s}$, east. 2. Here $\Delta v = v_f - v_i = 40 \frac{m}{s}$, east $- 60 \frac{m}{s}$, west $= 40 \frac{m}{s}$, east $+ 60 \frac{m}{s}$, east $= +100 \frac{m}{s}$, east.

(Note that velocities are written as $\frac{m}{s}$, rather than m/s. When you place units or numbers that should be in the denominator in the same line as the numerator, there is always a chance of mixing up the numbers on a test.)

We often use coordinate axes to give directions to velocities, changes in velocities, and accelerations.

TIME TO TRY

Let west be the positive direction of the coordinate axis. Answer questions 1 and 2 from the previous Quick Check with + for west and – for east.

Answers: 1. $\Delta v = v_f - v_i = +40\,\dfrac{m}{s} - \left(+60\,\dfrac{m}{s}\right) = -20\,\dfrac{m}{s}$.

2. $\Delta v = v_f - v_i = -40\,\dfrac{m}{s} - \left(+60\,\dfrac{m}{s}\right) = -100\,\dfrac{m}{s}$.

Acceleration is the ratio of the change in velocity to the time interval over which the velocity changed. For example, $a = \dfrac{+40\,\dfrac{m}{s}}{20\,s} = +2\,\dfrac{m}{s^2}$.

✔ **QUICK CHECK**

Find the accelerations in questions 1 and 2 from the previous Quick Check. (All necessary information is already given.)

Answers: 1. $a = \dfrac{\Delta v}{\Delta t} = \dfrac{-20\,\dfrac{m}{s}}{60\,s} = -\dfrac{1}{3}\,\dfrac{m}{s^2}$, or $a = +\dfrac{1}{3}\,\dfrac{m}{s^2}$, east.

2. $a = \dfrac{\Delta v}{\Delta t} = \dfrac{-100\,\dfrac{m}{s}}{240\,s} = -0.42\,\dfrac{m}{s^2}$ or $a = +0.42\,\dfrac{m}{s^2}$, east.

Why didn't we need to state that the direction was west in each initial answer, but needed to include east in the second version? Also, Joey could have changed direction in two different ways. Can you figure out what they are?

In your physics course, you will study accelerations that occur when the direction of the velocity changes. For now, you've gotten the basic ideas and definitions here.

PRACTICE

Here are a number of problems for practice in working with displacements, velocities, and accelerations.

1. The positions of a car on a test track at the beginning and end of a 5 s time interval follow. The track is in an east-west direction with distances increasing to the west. Here the symbol "y" is used to represent displacement. Calculate the average velocity for each of the following examples:

   a) $y_1 = 20$ m; $y_2 = 20$ m
   b) $y_1 = 20$ m; $y_2 = 40$ m
   c) $y_2 = 40$ m; $y_1 = 40$ m
   d) $y_1 = 40$ m; $y_2 = 20$ m

2. The average velocities of a car on a test track are given at the beginning and end of a 5 s time interval. Calculate the average acceleration in each of the following cases:

   a) $v_1 = 10\frac{m}{s}$, E; $v_2 = 40\frac{m}{s}$, E.
   b) $v_1 = 40\frac{m}{s}$, E; $v_2 = 10\frac{m}{s}$, E.

   c) $v_1 = 10\frac{m}{s}$, W; $v_2 = 40\frac{m}{s}$, W.
   d) $v_1 = 40\frac{m}{s}$, W; $v_2 = 10\frac{m}{s}$, W.

   e) $v_1 = 10\frac{m}{s}$, E; $v_2 = 40\frac{m}{s}$, W.
   f) $v_1 = 40\frac{m}{s}$, E; $v_2 = 10\frac{m}{s}$, W.

   g) $v_1 = 10\frac{m}{s}$, W; $v_2 = 40\frac{m}{s}$, E.
   h) $v_1 = 40\frac{m}{s}$, W; $v_2 = 10\frac{m}{s}$, E.

   i) $v_1 = 10\frac{m}{s}$, E; $v_2 = 10\frac{m}{s}$, W.
   j) $v_1 = 40\frac{m}{s}$, W; $v_2 = 40\frac{m}{s}$, E.

3. A car is headed to the right on a road as you stand alongside the road. Call the direction to the right positive and the direction to the left negative. Explain what will happen to the car in each of the following circumstances:

   a) velocity positive; acceleration positive
   b) velocity positive; acceleration negative
   c) velocity negative; acceleration positive
   d) velocity negative; acceleration negative

Answers: 1. a) $\Delta y = 0$; $v_{avg} = 0$; b) $\Delta y = 20$ m; $v_{avg} = +4\frac{m}{s}$; c) $\Delta y = 0$; $v_{avg} = 0$. d) $\Delta y = -20$ m; $v_{avg} = -4\frac{m}{s}$. 2. a) $\Delta v = 30\frac{m}{s}$, E; $a_{avg} = 6\frac{m}{s^2}$, E. b) $\Delta v = -30\frac{m}{s}$, E; $a_{avg} = 6\frac{m}{s^2}$, W; c) $\Delta v = 30\frac{m}{s}$, W; $a_{avg} = 6\frac{m}{s^2}$, W. d) $\Delta v = -30\frac{m}{s}$, W; $a_{avg} = 6\frac{m}{s^2}$, E.

3. In two of these the velocity is increasing in magnitude and in two it is decreasing in magnitude. Hint: It is not decreasing in magnitude in (d) because the change in velocity is in the same direction as the velocity.

e) $\Delta v = 40 \frac{m}{s} - \left(-10 \frac{m}{s}\right) = 50 \frac{m}{s}$; W; $a_{avg} = 10 \frac{m}{s^2}$. W.

f) $\Delta v = 10 \frac{m}{s} - \left(-40 \frac{m}{s}\right) = 50 \frac{m}{s}$; W; $a_{avg} = 10 \frac{m}{s^2}$. W.

g) $\Delta v = 50 \frac{m}{s}$; E; $a_{avg} = 10 \frac{m}{s^2}$. E. h) $\Delta v = 50 \frac{m}{s}$; E; $a_{avg} = 10 \frac{m}{s^2}$. E.

i) $\Delta v = 20 \frac{m}{s}$; E; $a_{avg} = 4 \frac{m}{s^2}$; E; j) $\Delta v = 80 \frac{m}{s}$; E; $a_{avg} = 16 \frac{m}{s^2}$. E.

Forces

We know that forces may cause change. A push or a pull is an example of a **force**, but gravitational attractions, which occur without direct contact, are also forces. We've experienced pushes, shoves, punches in the arm, and the difficulty in pushing a stalled car off the road. In August 2008, 30 bystanders in the Bronx, New York, lifted a bus off a woman. The difficulty in pushing a car or lifting a bus shows that there is a built-in resistance to change in motion. Our name for the built-in resistance—we can use a fancy word and call it "innate resistance"—is *inertial mass*, though we usually just call it "mass." Instinct also tells us that a force acting on a mass that is free to move results in a change of motion, an acceleration of that mass. Weight is the name for the attractive force that the Earth exerts on another body when that force is measured with a scale. We'll start with mass, and then define force by connecting acceleration with force and mass.

MASS

You are buying lemons in the supermarket. You want a juicy lemon. How would you compare two lemons in order to decide which one to buy?

You could find a scale, but many supermarkets have removed scales from their produce sections. Or you could hold one lemon in each hand and see which feels the heaviest. That's a very primitive kind of balance procedure. A knife-edge balance, such as that shown in Figure 3.3, lets us compare an unknown mass with a known mass.

FIGURE 3.3   A knife-edge balance.

Although balances actually compare weights, mass is proportional to weight at the Earth's surface. A mass of 1 kg corresponds to a weight of 2.2 pounds at sea level.

We've already noticed that acceleration is proportional to force. When more than one force acts on a body, its acceleration is proportional to the net or resultant force that sums up the action of all the external forces acting on that body or system. We've also noticed that the greater the mass of a body, the more resistance there is to change of motion of that body. This means that the acceleration is *inversely proportional* to the mass. Write an equation that states that acceleration, *a*, is proportional to external force, F^{ext}, and inversely proportional to mass, *m*.

Answer: You should have written $a = \dfrac{F^{ext}}{m}$. You may have seen this written as $F^{ext} = ma$, but the version $a = \dfrac{F^{ext}}{m}$ helps remind us of the physical reasoning behind the law. In either form, this equation is known as **Newton's Second law**.

We get the unit of force, the **Newton**, N, by multiplying the units of mass and acceleration: $1\,\text{N} = 1\,\text{kg} \times 1\,\dfrac{\text{m}}{\text{s}^2} = 1\,\dfrac{\text{kg}\cdot\text{m}}{\text{s}^2}$. Like the kilogram, the second (s) is a basic unit by definition, but the meter (m) is found from the definition of the velocity of light. Nonetheless, we can think of the kilogram, meter, and second as our three basic units. We won't need additional basic units until we deal with topics such as electricity or thermodynamics.

WEIGHT

You probably have a good idea of what weight is. Define weight for yourself and then check the following definition.

Weight is another one of those words, like gravity, that has been taken into physics from everyday speech. It has turned out to be a dangerous crossover. We know that the Earth interacts with bodies on its surface because the mysterious force "gravity" is said to pull objects toward the Earth. (It's not at all obvious that the objects also pull on the Earth, but they do.) This gravitational interaction gives rise to the force that we call weight. A small part of this force is used to keep an object at the surface from flying off into space by following its natural tendency to move in a straight line, but most of this force gives rise to what a scale measures. We may think of the weight of an object as this downward force that the Earth exerts on an object. When the object and scale are at rest, the scale exerts a force of the same magnitude back on the object. This force is proportional to the mass of the object, so we write $W = mg$, where g is the acceleration the downward gravitational force W gives to a body of mass m at the surface of the Earth.

Weight is the net downward force that the Earth exerts on an object as measured by a scale. ■

NEWTON'S LAWS OF MOTION

Isaac Newton developed three important laws that describe force and mass.

NEWTON'S THIRD LAW See what you might already understand about Newton's Third law:

Andrew shoves Jim and Jim falls. Which statement correctly describes the situation while Andrew is shoving Jim?

a) Andrew's hand exerts a force on Jim, but Jim's body does not exert a force back on Andrew's hand.

b) Jim's body exerts a force back on Andrew's hand, but it is not as big as the force Andrew's hand exerts on Jim.

c) Jim's body exerts exactly as large a force on Andrew's hand as Andrew's hand exerts on Jim's body.

d) Jim's body exerts a larger a force on Andrew's hand than the force Andrew's hand exerts on Jim's body.

Answer: (c). This may seem absurd, but forces of the same magnitude have very different results on different objects. Andrew used a frictional force of the Earth on his feet to avoid falling, while Jim, caught unawares, didn't have time to resist.

As Newton's Third law states, *In any interaction between two bodies, each one exerts a force of the same magnitude on the other.* If the force is a pull, each pulls on the other. If the force is a push, each pushes the other away. Another way of stating this is to say that the two forces, one on each body, have opposite directions.

NEWTON'S FIRST LAW If you place a book and a ball on a level, smooth table, what do you expect them to do? Why?

Answer: If we assume that we do not have a trick ball or a hollowed-out book with a mechanism built into it, then we expect the ball and book to sit there. We know that we have to do something to make them move.

If you have a friend who is on a trip place a ball and book on a table in the dining car of a railroad train, what would you see if you could look through the window into the train? Why?

Answer: With the same assumptions as in the previous setting, and the additional assumption that the train moves very smoothly, that is, at constant velocity, we expect to see the book and ball at rest on the table. The person in the train would need to do something to the ball and book to make them move.

Roughly stated, if a system, such as ourselves and our surroundings, is not moving, the system starts to move only when an outside (external) force is exerted on it. This also holds true for changes in velocity in a system that is initially moving at constant velocity relative to us when we are at rest. (Note: An object cannot move itself, but a person in the room can produce the external force on an object.) As Newton's First law explains, *An object remains in a state of rest or a state of motion at constant velocity unless made to change that state by a net force.*

PICTURE THIS

You are standing in the aisle of a bus or subway train at rest. Then it starts moving with the greatest possible acceleration. What happens to your body? Why?

Answer: If you don't dig your feet into the floor quickly and hard, you will probably fall over. Your body wants to stay where it is. (We concluded previously that it takes an outside force to make a body change its position.) If the frictional force the floor exerts on your feet is not large enough to give you the same acceleration as the bus or train, your body won't be able to move with it.

An object remains at rest when its surroundings remain at rest. An object moves at constant velocity when it is part of a system moving at constant velocity. It takes a net external force on an object to make it accelerate. That force may come from bodies inside or outside the system, but not from the object itself. ▮

Let's work through some examples applying Newton's laws of motion:

WORKED EXAMPLE 3.2

1. You place a marble on a kitchen counter. What will happen to it? Why? Are there any external forces on the marble? If so, what are they?

The marble will sit there if the counter is level. Newton's First law tells us that any external forces on the marble must add up to zero. We know that the interaction between the Earth and the marble results in a downward force on the marble. For the sum of forces to be zero, a force of equal magnitude in the opposite direction must be exerted on the marble by the countertop. This is shown in Figure 3.4. Whenever an object is at rest despite the presence of a known force, Newton's First law lets us deduce that at least one other external force is acting on the object. Remember that Newton's First law is particularly useful when objects are at rest or moving at constant velocity.

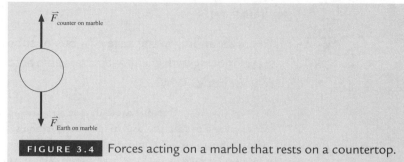

FIGURE 3.4   Forces acting on a marble that rests on a countertop.

2. You place the same marble on a ramp for handicapped access to a building. What will happen to the marble? Why? Are there any external forces on the marble? If so, what are they?

This is a no-brainer: The marble will roll down the ramp. Because the marble interacts with the Earth, a portion of the force of the Earth on the marble acts parallel to the ramp. The rest of the force that the Earth exerts on the marble is balanced by a force the ramp exerts on the marble. This is shown in Figures 3.5a and 3.5b.

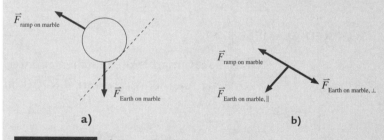

FIGURE 3.5   **a)** Forces acting on a marble on a ramp. **b)** Components of the force that the Earth exerts on the marble.

Figure 3.5a shows that the two forces do not sum to zero. Figure 3.5b shows the force of the Earth on the marble broken up into two components, one parallel to the ramp and the other perpendicular to the ramp. We can see that $\vec{F}_{\text{ramp on marble}}$ is equal and opposite to $\vec{F}_{\text{Earth on marble, }\perp}$, while $\vec{F}_{\text{Earth on marble, }\parallel}$ is a net external force on the marble. Figure 3.5a is a force diagram. Figure 3.5b is a free body diagram. In a free body diagram, we show the forces, but the body has been reduced to the point where the tails of the vector arrows representing the forces meet.

3. You hold the marble in your hand and open your hand so the marble is released. What will happen to the marble? Why? Are there any external forces on the marble? If so, what are they?

The marble will fall because of the pull of the Earth on the marble. It goes from a state in which it is not moving to a state in which it is moving at constantly increasing velocity. (This is not obvious because it falls so fast, but you can see the increase in the velocity when you let the marble roll down a ramp with a gentle slope.) The external force on the marble is the force of gravity, the pull that the Earth exerts on the marble. There also is a tiny buoyant force from the air and a force of resistance from the air, but in introductory courses we ignore those most of the time.

Work and Energy

PICTURE THIS

Suppose you had to spend the day working at a plant nursery in a job where you had to put 50-pound bags of topsoil in cars and pickups all day. You would probably say that you had done a full day's work. Let's look at this situation:

Use what we just learned about Newton's First and Third laws to describe the forces on your hands by a bag of topsoil and on the bag of topsoil by your hands.

The Earth pulls down on the topsoil with a force that we call the force of gravity on the bag of topsoil.

1. If the topsoil is to move up at constant velocity, your hands must be exerting an equal and opposite force on the topsoil.

   Which of Newtons' laws are we using here?

2. If your hands exert a force on the topsoil, then the topsoil is exerting an equal and opposite force on your hands.

   Which of Newton's laws are we using here?

Answers: 1. The first law 2. The third law

Is it easier to lift the bag a shorter distance onto the back of a pickup or a greater distance over the side of the pickup truck?

It's always harder to lift the bag a greater distance. Some of that has to do with how high we have to reach and the structure of our bodies, but when lifting with our arms in front it is harder to lift a heavy weight a greater distance.

We define the **work** done when the force and displacement are in the same direction as $W = Fd$, where W is work, F is force, and d is displacement. When the force and displacement are in opposite directions we take the work to be negative. We will later learn that we have to modify this definition to take into account any angle between the force and the displacement, but this equation will be enough to "work" with for now.

The unit of work, the **Joule**, is the product of the units of force and displacement, so $1 \text{ J} = 1 \text{ N} \cdot \text{m} = 1 \dfrac{\text{kg} \cdot \text{m}^2}{\text{s}^2}$. This same unit is used for all types of energy.

✔ **QUICK CHECK**

1. Is the work you do in lifting a 50-pound bag 2 feet positive or negative?

2. Is the work the bag does on your hands positive or negative?

Answers: 1. The force you exert on the bag and its displacement are parallel and in the same direction, which means the work is positive. Therefore you do 100 foot-pounds of work on the bag. 2. The force the bag exerts on your hands and the displacement of your hands are in opposite directions, which means the work is negative. Therefore the bag does minus 100 foot-pounds of work on your hands. We say that you have supplied 100 foot-pounds of energy to the bag.

In order to get a 50-pound bag moving as you lift it, you have to accelerate it by applying a force opposite to and greater than the force of gravity to the bag. You could let the bag slow down when it reaches the highest point by letting gravity pull on it. But until you do that, the bag has the energy you gave it to start it moving. That energy it has while moving is called kinetic energy. It turns out that a consistent definition of **kinetic energy** is $K = \dfrac{1}{2}mv^2$, where K is kinetic energy, m is mass, and v is the magnitude of the velocity.

Now suppose you were lifting a large bag of gravel and let it drop on your toe. Ouch! That bag could break a toe or two. It could do work on your toes as a result of where it had been: lifted up so that it could pick up speed while falling. What makes the bag pick up speed? The interaction of the bag with the Earth. We say that the bag has **gravitational potential energy**, because the force of gravity pulling it toward the surface of the Earth can do work on the bag during its displacement.

A compressed spring can exert a force on an object and do work on that object. A person with a pocket knife is in great danger if he or she gets too close to a powerful magnet. A person who gets too close to the edge of a cliff may die of the fall. Whenever the configuration of objects is such that they will attract or repel one another unless restrained, begin to move and pick up kinetic energy because of work the forces do, we say the system of objects has potential energy. Our three examples have elastic (spring) potential energy, magnetic potential energy, and gravitational potential energy.

Now we are ready to introduce the relation between work and energy:

The sum of all types of energy at the beginning time plus work done by a force external to the system over the time interval is equal to the sum of all types of energy at the end of the time interval.

This is known as the **law of conservation of energy**.

Remember that work can be negative as well as positive, so the total energy at the end can be less than the total energy at the beginning. That result can occur when the object doing the work is not part of the system.

✔ **QUICK CHECK**

A bag of topsoil is lying on the ground. Set gravitational potential energy to zero at ground level. (Only changes in gravitational potential energy are meaningful, because no motion occurs unless the relative positions change. When h is the height above ground level, the usual convention is to set gravitational potential energy equal to mgh). State whether the kinetic energy K of the bag, the gravitational potential energy U of the bag-Earth system, and the work that has been done on the bag by the force of gravity are positive, negative, or zero at the following times:

1. At $t = 0$ s the bag is lying on the ground.

2. At $t = 1$ s the bag is 1 ft above the ground and is moving upward at 1 ft per s.

3. At $t = 2$ s the bag is 2 ft above the ground; you are holding it in your arms but have not yet moved to put it in the pickup truck.

4. At $t = 4$ s the bag is lying in the pickup truck.

Answers: 1. $K = U_g = W = 0$. 2. K is positive—the bag is moving, U_g is positive—the bag is above ground level. W is positive—you have done work on the bag to start it moving and to lift it at constant velocity. 3. $K = 0$—the bag is not moving, $U_g > 0$—the bag has been raised above ground level. $W > 0$—the work was done over the whole time interval while you were raising the bag. 4. $K = 0$—the bag is not moving. $U_g > 0$—the bag is above ground level. $W > 0$—the work was done over the whole time interval while you were raising the bag.

Subtle point: When we start to write equations we can include either the work done by the force of gravity on the bag or the gravitational potential energy of the bag-Earth system. If we include both we will be counting gravity twice. Another way of saying this is that we either use the force model or the energy model, but have to be careful not to use the two together for the same interaction. The following section will help to make this clear. ▪

WORK-ENERGY BAR CHARTS A work-energy bar chart is a visual mnemonic (for memorization) device that lets you keep track of the different forms of energy that belong to a system of objects. Once you have drawn a correct work-energy bar chart, the writing of the equivalent equation is trivial. (When we discuss problem-solving in Chapter 5, we will pay much more attention to defining our system.)

Say you are pulling a sled with a child on board. Define the sled and child as the system. Draw a dashed outline to mark out the system (Figure 3.6). In this case the rope is exerting an external force on the system. The rope is doing work on the system either to get the sled moving initially, or against friction while the sled moves at a constant speed. If

Forces acting on a pulled sled.

we do not include the surface of the snow in the system, friction is an external force that does negative work.

On a work-energy bar chart there is a location for each type of energy at the initial time and for each type of energy at the final time of the situation depicted. Bars representing work are shown between the initial and final forms of energy because work occurs over a period of time. Figure 3.7 shows what the work-energy bar chart for this example should look like.

The first bar in Figure 3.7 represents any kinetic energy the sled has at the time we pick as the initial time. The second bar represents the work done on the sled by the external force exerted by the rope tied to the sled. Because this work is done over a period of time before the final time, the bar is placed to the left of the equal sign. The third bar, representing the work done by friction, is also placed to the left of the equal sign because this work too occurs before the final time. By summing the positive and negative heights of the bars to the left of the equal sign, we arrive at the bar for the kinetic energy at the final time. Even when a problem has not yet been solved numerically, the heights of the bars should be your best estimate of the size of each type of energy and work.

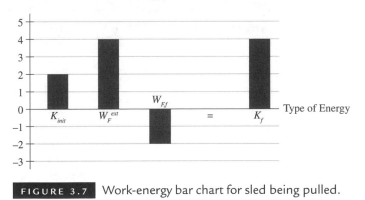

FIGURE 3.7 Work-energy bar chart for sled being pulled.

WORKED EXAMPLE 3.3

A 2.00 kg mass is thrown downward with a 5.00 $\frac{m}{s}$ initial speed from the 3 m high roof of a house and hits the ground. Use $g = 10 \frac{m}{s^2}$ for simplicity. The initial time is when the mass leaves the hand. The final time is the instant when it has stopped moving. Consider the Earth as part of the system, and take the force of friction as being internal to the system. That means that any energy that ends up as thermal energy at the end of the process must have its own bar in the final state. Call that bar $\Delta U_{\text{int. thermal}}$. Because the Earth is part of the system, the relative positions of the mass and the Earth are accounted for in the gravitational potential energy. Construct two work-energy bar charts for this system. First construct a qualitative bar chart without showing any energy values. Then construct bars proportional to the magnitudes of the various types of energy. Use the bars shown in Figure 3.8.

$$\overline{\quad} \quad \overline{\quad} \quad \overline{\quad} \quad = \quad \overline{\quad} \quad \overline{\quad} \quad \overline{\quad}$$
$$K_i \qquad U_{g,i} \quad W \qquad K_f \qquad U_{g,f} \quad \Delta U_{\text{int. thermal}}$$

FIGURE 3.8 Bars represented in a typical work-energy bar chart for a falling mass.

Answer: Only the second bar chart, with actual quantities, is shown. Your first bar chart should have been similar to this. Because K_i is 25 J, and *mgh* is 60 J, the internal thermal energy at the end is 85 J. Figure 3.9 shows what the correct bar chart looks like. It must be emphasized that you often will just draw bars of relative sizes and use the types of energy you have to determine what to calculate.

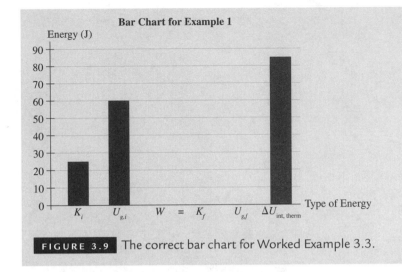

Bar Chart for Example 1

FIGURE 3.9   The correct bar chart for Worked Example 3.3.

WORKED EXAMPLE 3.4

A 2.00 kg mass is placed at the top of a 15.0° incline, then given a quick shove so that it starts down the incline at 5.00 $\frac{m}{s}$. The mass moves a vertical distance of 3.00 m before coming to a stop. Consider the Earth as part of the system, and take the force of friction as being internal to the system as in Worked Example 3.3. Construct a work-energy bar chart for this system. Use the bars shown in Figure 3.10.

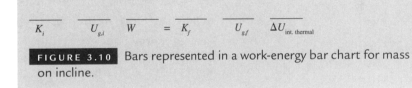

FIGURE 3.10   Bars represented in a work-energy bar chart for mass on incline.

Answer: Your work-energy bar chart should have looked like Figure 3.11:

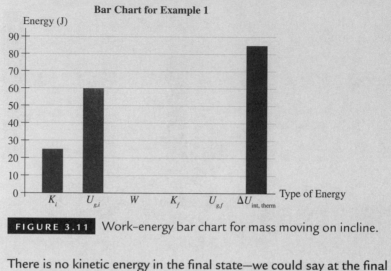

Bar Chart for Example 1

FIGURE 3.11 Work–energy bar chart for mass moving on incline.

There is no kinetic energy in the final state—we could say at the final time—because the mass has stopped moving.

TIME TO TRY

1. A 65 kg skater, originally moving at 20 $\frac{m}{s}$, comes to a stop after gliding a distance of 100 m on a rough sidewalk. Draw a work-energy bar chart showing her energies at the beginning and end of the glide. Note: This bar chart will look the same whether or not you include the Earth in your system because the gravitational potential energy does not change.

2. A 60 kg skater, originally moving at 30 $\frac{m}{s}$, glides up a 50 m long 30° incline. (Can you use trigonometry to show that her vertical ascent is 25 m?) Draw a work-energy bar chart showing her energies at the beginning and end of the glide. Do not include the Earth in your system.

3. Draw a second bar chart for the skater in question 2, but this time include the Earth in your system.

Answers: 1. Here is the work-energy bar chart for question 1.

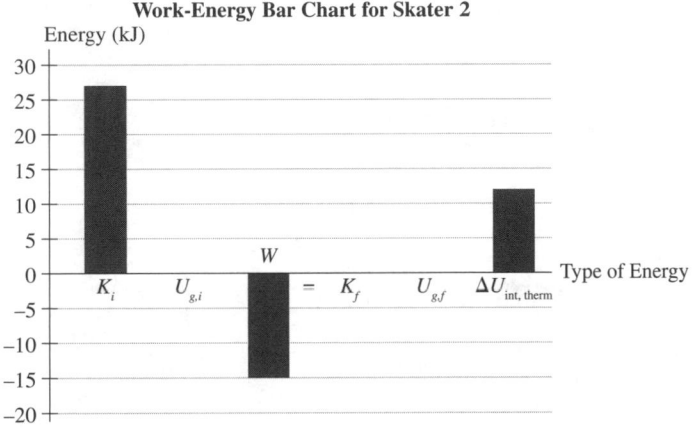

Work-Energy Bar Chart for Skater 1

FIGURE 3.12 The work-energy bar chart for Skater 1.

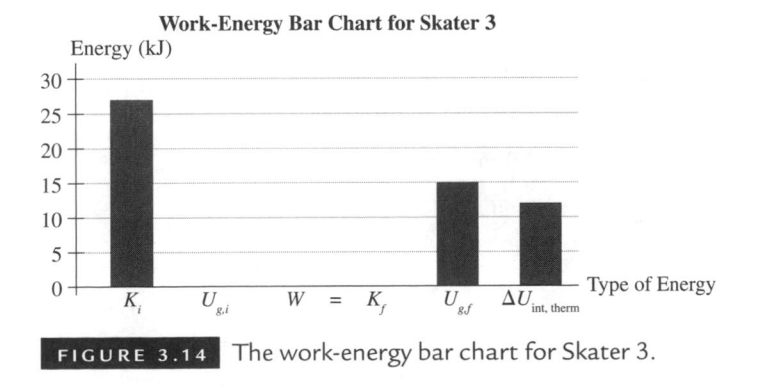

Work-Energy Bar Chart for Skater 2

FIGURE 3.13 The work-energy bar chart for Skater 2.

Work-Energy Bar Chart for Skater 3

FIGURE 3.14 The work-energy bar chart for Skater 3.

PRACTICE

1. A friend drops a ball from a dorm window. The ball falls from a height of 21.0 m and is caught by your hand at a height of 1.00 m. Use $g = 10 \frac{m}{s^2}$. The initial time is the instant when the ball is released and the final time is when the ball stops moving. Draw a work-energy bar chart for the ball. (Hint: What is the initial velocity of a ball that is "dropped"?)

2. You throw a ball straight up. It leaves your hand with an initial velocity of $40 \frac{m}{s}$. The final time is when the ball is at the highest point it reaches. Use $g = 10 \frac{m}{s^2}$. Draw a work-energy bar chart for the ball. (Hint: What is the velocity of the ball at the highest point?)

3. You throw a ball straight up. It leaves your hand with an initial velocity of $40 \frac{m}{s}$. The final time is when the ball has fallen back into your hand. Use $g = 10 \frac{m}{s^2}$. Draw a work-energy bar chart for the ball. (Hint: What has happened to the kinetic energy your hand gave to the ball after it has fallen back into your hand?)

Final Stretch!

Now that you have finished reading this chapter it is time to stretch your brain and check how much you have learned.

RUNNING WORDS

Here are the terms introduced in this chapter. Write them in a notebook and define them in your own words. Then go back through the chapter to check on their meanings, and on any formulas associated with them. Make corrections as needed and try to list examples of the use of each term.

Position	Newton Second law
Change of position	Newton's Third law
Distance	Kinetic energy
Displacement	Work
Speed	Gravitational poten-
Velocity	tial energy
Change in velocity	Energy conservation
Delta	Work-energy bar chart
Acceleration	Newton
Force	Joule
Newton's First law	Weight

WEB RESOURCES

For additional help, enter any of the topics listed under "What did you learn?" or any bold-face section title in a Web search engine. Check through a number of sites to find one at the right level.

■ *One site with a simulation applicable to this chapter is*

http://phet.colorado.edu/simulations/sims.php?sim=The_Moving_Man

The Phet site was designed by a group working under Nobel prize winner Carl Wieman at the University of Colorado, and will be of help to you when taking your physics courses.

4 Physics Concepts, Part II

When you complete this chapter you should be able to:

■ Explain how to define and/or calculate the following:

- Forces between like and unlike charges
- Conductors and insulators
- Charge polarization and induction
- Coulomb's law
- Electric field
- Electric potential energy and electric potential
- Ohm's law
- North and south magnetic poles
- Temperature and thermal energy
- Thermometers and temperature scales
- Zeroth and First laws of thermodynamics
- Oscillation, period, frequency, and amplitude
- Light ray and shadow
- Diffraction
- Structure of an atom and atomic nucleus

Electricity

Humans have been giving names to things for a very long time. Our ancestors named plants, trees, animals, themselves, and processes such as eating, running, or hunting. They named lightning and attributed it to the gods of their tribes: Zeus, Thor, and Jehovah. For all we know, some scientific observations may have occurred over and over but were not recorded until writing was invented. What we do know is that someone noticed that a piece of amber rubbed with fur could attract and lift up bits of pith that came from a reed. What is so significant about this attraction is that it is the exact opposite of gravity. Here was a contradictory phenomenon, and it was named for amber, *elektron* in Greek.

Electricity is a property of amber, and, as we now know, of the protons and electrons contained in all atoms. It is a name for a property we observe, not an explanation of how it occurs. All we can do is describe how "electrical"—we now say electrically charged—particles behave. Just as inertial mass is a property that describes how a force is needed to change the velocity of a mass, electric charge is a property that lets particles and the objects that contain those particles exhibit electrical attraction and repulsion. Any two electrically charged particles exert long-range forces on one another—repulsive when the particles have charges of the same sign, attractive when the particles have charges of the opposite sign. Just as masses do not need to be in contact with the Earth to be attracted by it, the objects exhibiting electrical attraction and repulsion do not need to make contact with each other.

In addition, because all bodies are made up of positively and negatively charged particles, a neutral body—one in which the charges sum to zero—can be attracted by a body with a net charge because the particles in the neutral body shift so that there is a net opposite charge closer to the charged particle. This property, called charge polarization, is similar to the shift of mass by gravity, a shift known as the tides. See the further discussion of induction starting on page 147.

Your Starting Point

You have probably studied the structure of atoms in a high school chemistry course or in general science. Some of you may have some experience with physics as well. Try the following questions:

1. What is the structure of a single atom?

2. What particles can be found inside an atomic nucleus?

Answers: 1. Every atom contains a very highly compact nucleus that contains most of the mass of the atom. Outside the nucleus there are electrons that can be thought of as moving around the nucleus in orbits of varying shapes and sizes, mostly very far out compared to the diameter of the nucleus. (When you study quantum mechanics you will learn that this is a simplistic model.) 2. The nucleus contains protons, positively-charged particles, and neutrons, particles with no net electrical charge.

PICTURE THIS

You can check out the properties of static electricity at home.

Experiment 1: Take about 8 inches of cellophane tape, the cheap stuff that sticks, not the more expensive tape. Fold over a bit at an end so you can hold on to it without it sticking to you, and place the tape on a wooden or plastic desk or table. Press it down firmly and prepare a second piece of tape the same way. Then pull them up fairly quickly and bring them close together. What do the two pieces of tape do? (Note: This may not work properly if there is too much humidity in the air, because water molecules can pick the charges off the tape.)

Answer: _____

Experiment 2: Prepare two strips of tape, but now place one piece on top of the other. Pull the two pieces of tape off the tabletop together, then pull them apart. When you now bring them close together, what do you observe?

Answer: _____

You should have observed the two pieces of tape repelling one another in the first experiment and attracting one another in the second experiment. The friction generated in the act of pulling causes some separation of charge. We now have to explain why we see both attraction and repulsion. Other ways of preparing charged bodies include rubbing a glass rod with silk or a rubber rod with fur. After rubbing, one glass rod can repel another glass rod, silk repels silk, rubber repels rubber, and fur repels fur. However, glass attracts rubber and silk attracts fur.

CONDUCTORS AND INSULATORS

After many experiments, scientists in the past found that all charged bodies either attracted or repelled one another. Later experiments measured the strengths of these forces. The results show that there are two kinds of the electrical property called **charge**: one called **positive charge** and the other called **negative charge**. Benjamin Franklin assigned the name positive to the charge of the glass rod, and that name has stuck ever since.

If you can estimate the weight of one of your pieces of tape and the angle it makes with the vertical when near another piece of tape, you can compare the electrical force to the force of gravity. A very rough estimate would be that the electrical force is of the same order of magnitude as the force of gravity. What you will learn in class is that the amount of charge causing that force is very small in comparison to the mass needed for the gravitational force.

Rough experiments show that more vigorous rubbing produces bodies that repel or attract more strongly. But the discovery that made precise experiments possible was that of **insulators** and **conductors**. Metals are examples of conductors: They not only conduct electricity well, they also conduct heat well. Wood and glass are examples of insulators: They do a good job of resisting the motion of charge through them. When a charged body is placed in contact with a conductor, it transfers some of its charge to the conductor. This charge spreads out all over the surface of the conductor.

✔ **QUICK CHECK**

Why does the charge spread out all over the conductor?

Answer: Because a charged body has one sign (one kind) of excess charge, the individual charged particles on the conductor all have the same type of charge, positive or negative. Because charges of the same type repel one another, they spread out as far as possible from one another.

We now know that the positively charged nuclei of atoms hardly move at all. It is a portion of the negatively charged electrons that is free to move in a conductor, toward a positively charged object, and away from a negatively charged object.

INDUCTION

We've seen how you can put electric charge on a body by friction, but there are other ways to charge a conductor.

CHARGE POLARIZATION   Before we can explain induction, we must look at how charges in a neutral body redistribute themselves when an object with a net electrical charge is brought close.

Suppose a conducting sphere is hanging by an insulating thread, as in Figure 4.1a, and that a positively charged rod is brought close as in Figure 4.1b.

We can show the distribution of positive and negative charges on the sphere in Figure 4.1a by indicating that positive and negative charges in equal quantities are distributed throughout the sphere as in Figure 4.2.

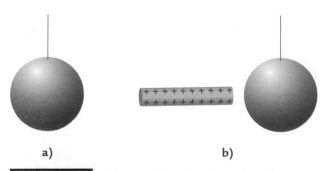

a)   b)

FIGURE 4.1   **a)** A neutral conducting sphere. **b)** A positively charged rod is brought close to the sphere.

FIGURE 4.2 The charge distribution in a neutral conducting sphere.

In the sphere in Figure 4.1b, the negative charges must have shifted toward the positively charged rod.

PICTURE THIS

Use the sphere in Figure 4.3 to sketch the charge distribution you expect to find in the sphere in Figure 4.1b.

FIGURE 4.3 Sketch the charge distribution in a sphere having a positively-charged rod at its left.

FIGURE 4.4 The charge distribution in a conducting sphere in the presence of a positive charge at its left.

Answer: You should have sketched something like this:

Something similar happens in insulators where the charges are fixed in place. There, however, the negative charges move only a little bit to the left and positive charges very, very slightly to the right, so that each atom remains electrically neutral individually. The shifts, however, still make the left side of the insulating sphere slightly negative and the right side slightly positive.

The shift of charge in a neutral conductor or insulator when in the presence of a charged body is known as charge polarization. ■

✔ **QUICK CHECK**

If the sphere is free to move when the charged rod is brought close to it, will the sphere remain hanging straight down or will it move. If it moves, in what direction will it move?

Answer: Because the charge on the side of the sphere closest to the rod is opposite to the charge on the rod, the sphere will move toward the rod until the horizontal electrical force is balanced by the horizontal component of the tension in the string.

Next we'll look at how charge polarization can be used to charge bodies without placing charges on them directly.

MORE ON INDUCTION

PICTURE THIS

You have two metal spheres hung by insulating threads. Bring positively charged metal sphere A up to metal sphere B so that they are close, but not touching, as in Figure 4.5a. As explained previously, B, even though uncharged, is attracted to A because of charge polarization. Then touch B with your finger as shown in Figure 4.5b. Predict what the state of B will be after you take your finger away and then remove Sphere A.

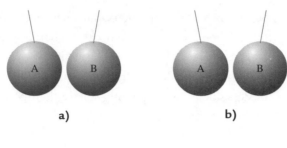

a)   b)

FIGURE 4.5 Charging by induction.

Answer: The Earth acts as a big conductor of electricity. The positive charge on A attracts the negative charge in B so the side of B near A becomes negatively charged, and the side of B opposite from A becomes positively charged, as in Figure 4.4. Because charge can move in a conductor—it's generally the electrons that are free to move—a neutral conductor can be attracted by a charged body as shown in Figure 4.5a.

When you touch B, electrons from the Earth can reach sphere B through your finger. When you remove your finger, the electrons remain on B because of the net positive charge on the right side of B that attracted them in the first place. This gives B an excess of negative charge that still remains when A is removed. We have charged B by **induction**, the charging of one object without touching it to a second charged object. Figure 4.6 shows how charge is distributed on Sphere B after the finger is removed.

FIGURE 4.6 The charge distribution on Sphere B after the finger has been removed.

TIME TO TRY

1. Two metal spheres hung by insulating threads repel one another. What can we say about any electric charge on the spheres?

2. Two rubber spheres hung by insulating threads repel one another. What can we say about any electric charge on the spheres?

3. Sphere A attracts sphere B and sphere C, but B and C neither attract nor repel one another. What can we say about any electric charge on the spheres?

Answers: 1. They are both charged and show the same type of charge, but we do not know what the sign of the charge is. 2. They are both charged and show the same type of charge, but we do not know what the sign of the charge is. (Insulators can hold charges on their surfaces or within their volume. They differ from conductors in two ways: The charges on an insulator cannot move around, only shift slightly like a person fidgeting in a chair, and charge can be present inside an insulator, not just on its surface.) 3. Sphere A is charged, but spheres B and C are both neutral (uncharged.)

QUANTITATIVE CONSIDERATIONS

If we place charge on a metal sphere, and touch that to an identical metal sphere, how much charge does each sphere now hold?

Answer: Our instinct tells us that like charges repel, and the only way that the charges can get as far from one another as possible is to spread out equally on the two spheres. That is correct. The distribution is not spherically symmetrical while the two spheres are touching, but there are equal amounts of charge on the two spheres. When they are separated by a large distance, each has a symmetrical distribution of one-half of the original charge.

How do we obtain two spheres with one-quarter of the original charge?

Answer: Touch one of the spheres with half the original charge to an identical sphere that is uncharged.

What has been described in these two questions is a physical equivalent to the mathematical operations by which a meter or an inch is halved, quartered, etc., so that we can construct rulers and meter sticks.

In principle, this allows us to experiment with charges of different magnitudes. In practice, such experiments are very difficult to carry out because charge leaks off charged bodies into the air.

WORKED EXAMPLE 4.1: DEDUCE A BASIC LAW FROM DATA

Table 4.1 gives the charges on two metal spheres and shows the forces they exert on one another at several distances. Use this table to deduce how the force depends on the charges on the bodies and on their center-to-center distances. The coulomb, symbol C , is the basic unit of charge. You are seeking a formula that relates charge q_1, charge q_2, the center-to-center distance of the charges, r, and a constant k. For instance, line 1 of Table 4.1 tells you that the magnitude of the constant is 9. (The formula you come up with will give you the units of the constant.) Ask yourself how you can get the numbers in the right hand column with 9 as the constant.

TABLE 4.1   Charges on spheres and forces the charges exert on one another.

Charge on Sphere 1 (μC)	Charge on Sphere 2 (μC)	Center-to-center distance (m)	Force each charge exerts on the other (mN)
1	1	1	9
2	2	1	36
3	3	1	81
1	2	1	18
1	3	1	27
2	3	1	54
1	1	2	2.25
1	1	3	1.00

Answer: Two 1-μC charges 1 m apart exert a 9×10^{-3} N force on one another. But a combination of a 1-μC and a 2-μC charge yields an 18×10^{-3} N force, while two 2-μC charges yield a 36×10^{-3} N force. Because $1 \times 1 \Rightarrow 9$, $1 \times 2 \Rightarrow 18$, $2 \times 2 \Rightarrow 36$, and $3 \times 3 \Rightarrow 81$, we conclude that the force in milliNewtons (mN) is equal to the product of the two charges times a constant 9, as long as the distance is itself held constant at 1 m. We can write $F \propto q_1 q_2$ by using the "proportional to" sign $\propto$. But we have $\frac{9}{4} = 2.25$ when the distance is doubled and $\frac{9}{9} = 1$ when the distance is tripled. The force is inversely proportional to the square of the distance r: $F \propto \frac{1}{r^2}$. If we put the two proportions together and add a constant of proportionality, k, we have **Coulomb's law:**

$$F \text{ (each charge on the other)} = \frac{k q_1 q_2}{r^2}$$

where $k = 9 \times 10^9 \frac{Nm^2}{C^2}$.

ANOTHER PICTURE: THE ELECTRIC FIELD

We will now find a way to find the force that a charged body fixed in place can exert on any other charge. When we complete these exercises we will be able to define a new concept, the **electric field**.

Figure 4.7 shows a 3-nC charge (1 nC $= 1 \times 10^{-9}$ C) fixed in place. It also shows four other points where we could locate another known charge, a "test charge." When we measure the force on the test charge, we determine how big a force the fixed charge can exert on it. Because we know Coulomb's law, we can predict the strength of the force. Assume that the fixed charge and the test charge are both positive charges. In that case the arrow at each point in Figure 4.7 shows the force on the test charge at that point. Note that each arrow points in the direction of the force on the test charge at that point. Its length is proportional to the magnitude (the strength) of the force. The tail of the arrow is located at the position of the test charge.

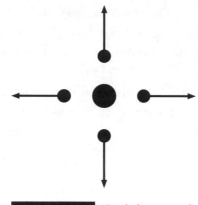

FIGURE 4.7 Fixed charge and test charges.

DEFINING THE ELECTRIC FIELD Next imagine that we take the ratio of the force to the magnitude of the test charge at each point. Because the test charge is small, the force is small. But when we divide the force by the test charge, a small number, the ratio is a larger number.

We want to draw arrows representing this *vector* ratio, $\dfrac{\vec{F}_{\text{on test charge}}}{q_{\text{test charge}}}$, in the same way we drew arrows for the forces in Figure 4.7. Do this below on the points where the test charge is located in Figure 4.8.

If you have sketched this correctly, your drawing should resemble, but not necessarily be exactly the same as, Figure 4.9.

The quantity that we represented symbolically in Figure 4.9, $\dfrac{\vec{F}_{\text{on test charge}}}{q_{\text{test charge}}}$, is known as the electric field, $\vec{E}$. We write that

FIGURE 4.8 A central charge with four points where a test charge may be located.

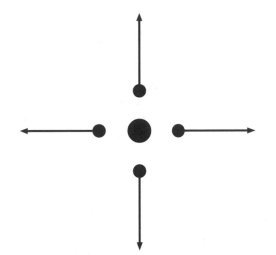

FIGURE 4.9 Arrows showing the ratio of force to test charge.

$\overrightarrow{E} = \dfrac{\overrightarrow{F}_{\text{on test charge}}}{q_{\text{test charge}}}$. Because a test charge will experience a force at any point at any distance from another charge, we say that there is an electric field in the space surrounding the fixed charge.

For any fixed charge, the arrows representing the electric field are larger when the test charge is closer and smaller when the test charge is farther out. All arrows point radially outward when we have a positive point fixed charge and a positive test charge, because like charges repel one another.

✔ **QUICK CHECK**

1. What happens to the size of the arrows representing the electric field when the points are closer to the fixed charge? Farther from the fixed charge?

2. What happens to the size of the arrows representing the electric field if the magnitude of the fixed charge is increased? Decreased?

3. What happens to the arrows representing the electric field if the sign of the fixed charge changes from positive to negative?

4. What happens to the size of the arrows representing the electric field if the magnitude of the test charge is increased? Decreased?

Answers: 1. The arrows are larger when the test charge is closer to the fixed charge, and smaller when the test charge is farther from the fixed charge, because the arrows represent the magnitude of the field as well as its direction. 2. All the arrows are proportionally larger when it increases and proportionally smaller when it decreases. 3. All the arrows point in the opposite direction because a negative fixed charge attracts positive test charges. 4. All the arrows stay the same. This will be explained next.

We are getting a picture of the forces that can be exerted by a fixed charge, but it would be great if we didn't have to draw a new diagram every time the test charge changed in magnitude. To avoid having to draw more than one diagram for a given source charge, we have taken the ratio of the force on the test charge at a point to the magnitude of the test charge: $\dfrac{\vec{F}_{\text{on test charge at point p}}}{q_{\text{test charge}}}$, and called that ratio the electric field at that point: $\vec{E}_{\text{at point p}} = \dfrac{\vec{F}_{\text{on test charge at point p}}}{q_{\text{test charge}}}$.

(To avoid sign confusion, we always use a positive test charge.)

✔ **QUICK CHECK**

Use Coulomb's law to calculate the electric field of a point charge.

1. Write Coulomb's law for the magnitude of the force, $F_{\text{fixed charge on test charge at point p}}$, that a fixed source charge, q_{fixed}, at the origin of coordinates exerts on a test charge, $q_{\text{test charge at point p}}$, at a distance, r, from the origin.

2. Find the ratio of that force to the fixed charge.

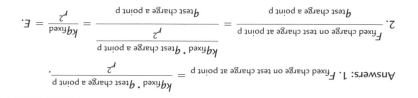

Answers: 1. $F_{\text{fixed charge on test charge at point p}} = \dfrac{kq_{\text{fixed}} \cdot q_{\text{test charge a point p}}}{r^2}$.

2. $\dfrac{F_{\text{fixed charge on test charge at point p}}}{q_{\text{test charge a point p}}} = \dfrac{\dfrac{kq_{\text{fixed}} \cdot q_{\text{test charge a point p}}}{r^2}}{q_{\text{test charge a point p}}} = \dfrac{kq_{\text{fixed}}}{r^2} = E$.

●

FIGURE 4.10 A fixed source charge.

The magnitude $E = |\vec{E}|$ of the electric field $\vec{E}$ at a point depends only on the fixed source charge. That's why we wanted to define it. For any test charge at a point where the electric field has magnitude E we get the magnitude of the force back by using $F_{\text{on test charge}} = q_{\text{test charge}}E_{\text{at point p}}$. If we want to include the directions of the force and the electric field we can use the vector equation $\vec{F}_{\text{on test charge}} = q_{\text{test charge}}\vec{E}_{\text{at point p}}$.

We only showed a small number of points in Figures 4.7 and 4.9. Imagine that there is one fixed positive source charge in Figure 4.10. Imagine placing a (positive) test charge anywhere. In what direction will the force on the test charge point? Draw some arrows representing the forces on test charges at different points.

Did you use your knowledge that two positive charges repel one another to draw arrows pointing radially outward? An example is shown in Figure 4.11, where we have drawn arrows from arbitrary points in place of the symmetric figures shown earlier.

✔ **QUICK CHECK**

Wherever there is a force, or a force would exist if a charge were there, there is an electric field present. We represent the electric field at a point with an arrow in the same way we represent a force with an arrow. However, if we note that there is an electric field pointing outward at every point along any radial line from the center, we can use a directed line to represent all these electric field vectors in a single direction. Try drawing such lines in Figure 4.12.

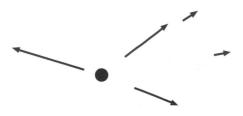

FIGURE 4.11 Force arrows pointing radially outward, greater for points closer to the source and smaller for points farther away.

●

FIGURE 4.12 A charge from which lines representing electric fields are to be drawn.

Did you draw lines radially outward from the source? Each such line is tangent to an infinite number of electric field vectors and represents all those vectors that start on points along the line. We call any line that is tangent to electric field vectors an **electric field line**. We indicate the directions of the electric field vectors by little arrows on the line, as in Figure 4.13.

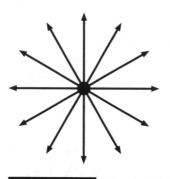

FIGURE 4.13 Electric field lines from a positive charge.

PRACTICE

1. Draw the electric field lines of a negative source charge. Use the charge shown in Figure 4.14.

2. Use what you now know about the electric field lines of positive and negative charges to draw the field lines of an equal positive and negative charge as shown in Figure 4.15.

⊖

FIGURE 4.14 The electric field lines of a negative charge.

⊖   ⊕

FIGURE 4.15 The electric field lines of a dipole, a positive and a negative charge of equal magnitude.

Answers. Figure 4.14 should show all the electric field lines drawn radially toward the center with the directions shown pointing inward, as shown in Figure 4.16. Figure 4.15 should show the electric field lines starting on the positive charge and ending on the negative charge, as shown in Figure 4.17. We say that a positive charge is a source for field lines and a negative charge is a sink for field lines.

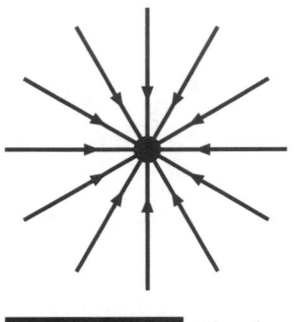

FIGURE 4.16 The electric field lines of a negative source charge.

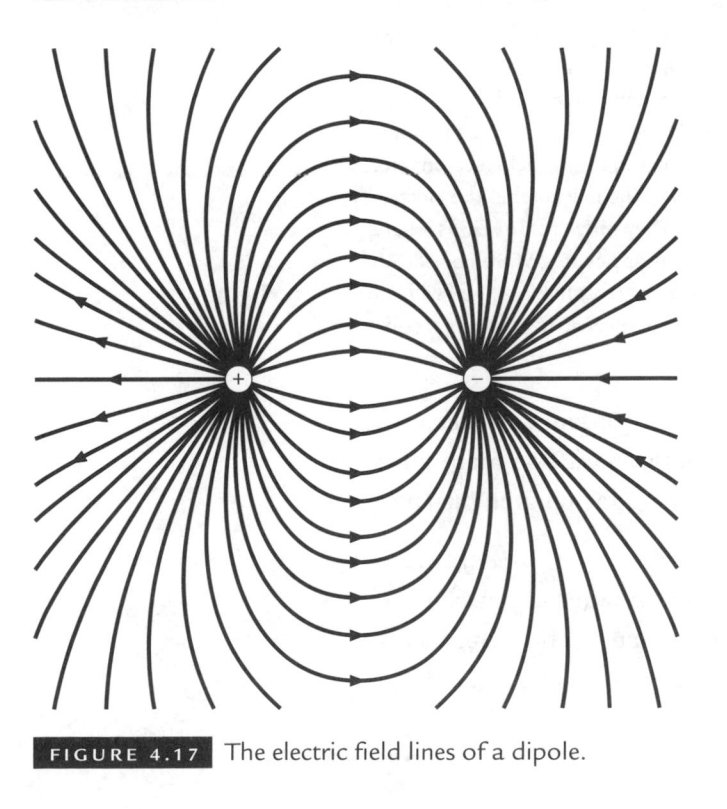

FIGURE 4.17 The electric field lines of a dipole.

TIME TO TRY

1. The Earth, shown as a sphere in Figure 4.18, has an excess of negative charge on it. Think about what we know about field lines for positive and negative point charges, and draw electric field lines for the Earth.

2. The field lines end at the surface of the Earth, a conductor. Why can't there be any charge inside a conductor; that is, why is all the charge on its surface?

Answer: 1. The field lines are exactly the same as those of a point negative charge, except that they end at the surface of the Earth rather than at its center. They point toward the Earth because the charge on the Earth is negative. 2. Like charges repel. Therefore, each individual charged particle placed on a conductor tries to get as far away from every other charged particle as possible. The only way for this to happen is for all the charge to be on the surface. Another way to look at this is to think about electric fields. If there were charges inside a conductor, there would be an electric field inside a conductor. Each charge's electric field would cause a repulsive force on every other particle of the same charge. If we place electrons on a metal, they repel electrons that are already in the metal. The electrons that are in the metal repel the electrons we just placed on it. Each has an electric field. They move to positions where their electric fields are paired up to be equal and opposite. (More correct, the vector sum of the electric fields inside the metal is zero.) In class, you will learn how to prove mathematically that there can be no electric field inside a conductor in an electrostatic situation.

FIGURE 4.18   Earth, a sphere with negative charge on its surface.

Summary:

1. Any two charged particles or bodies exert forces on one another. Particles of the same charge repel one another. Particles of opposite charge attract one another. For point particles the force that each particle exerts on the other is proportional to the product of the charges and inversely proportional to the square of the distance from each particle to the other (**Coulomb's law**).

2. We can picture this by drawing lines tangent to force directions on test charges brought near fixed charges. These **electric field lines**, a diagrammatic representation of force on each unit of charge (the fancy way of saying force per unit charge), point out from positive charges and in toward negative charges.

3. A body can become charged by friction, by receiving charge from another body that already has a charge on it, or by induction. We can charge a conductor by **induction**, because the presence nearby of a charged body induces a shift in the charges in a conductor. When grounded (placed in contact with a source of charge, usually a larger body), the conductor attracts charge opposite to that of the polarizing body from the ground.

ELECTRICAL ENERGY

Positive charges repel positive charges; negative charges repel negative charges; and positive and negative charges attract one another. If we allow two charged bodies to move freely, they will either move toward or away from one another. Either we have to do work on the charged bodies to separate them or force them together, or they can do work for us as they move toward or away from one another. We say that the **electrical potential energy** of the bodies increases when we have to do work on them because they will move back to their original positions while acquiring kinetic energy when released. We say that the bodies use up their electrical potential energy when their kinetic energy is increasing.

✔ QUICK CHECK

In each of the following examples, the charges either do work for us or we do work on them. For each example state whether work is done on or by the charges:

1. Two positive charges move toward one another. _____

2. Two positive charges move away from one another. _____

3. Two negative charges move toward one another. _____

4. Two negative charges move away from one another. _____

5. A negative and a positive charge move toward one another. _____

6. A negative and a positive charge move away from one another. _____

Answer: We do work on the charges in 1, 3, and 6. The charges can do work for us in 2, 4 and 5.

ELECTRICAL POTENTIAL

Electrical potential is the ratio of work done on one unit of positive charge to that positive charge when we move it closer to another positive charge. Because the unit of work is the joule and the unit of charge is the coulomb, the unit of electrical potential is the joule per coulomb, in magnitude the joules for each coulomb. Therefore the unit of potential, the **volt**, is given by $1 \text{ V} = \dfrac{1 \text{ J}}{1 \text{ C}}$.

That is not work per unit charge at a point, but work per unit charge over a distance when charge moves between two points. Likewise we can determine the amount of work done if we know the difference of potential between the two points. Formally, that **potential difference** is written as ΔV, but in sloppy yet common notation is often indicated as V and is called a "voltage." If the potential difference is positive, it means that the potential is increasing and we are approaching a positive charge or receding from a negative one. Because a potential difference is the work for each unit of charge that is moved, we only need to multiply the potential difference by the amount of charge to find out how much work has been done or has to be done: $W = q \times \Delta V$.

✔ **QUICK CHECK**

If +3.5 C is moved through a potential difference of +20 V, how much work is done on or by the charge?

Answer: To move +3.5 C toward a positive charge we must do work,
$W = q \times \Delta V = 3.5\ C \times 20\ V = 70\ V.$

OHM'S LAW Because the work done in each unit of time is power, the charge moving through a potential difference in a given time, a current, uses or supplies power. This relationship is explained by Ohm's Law.

Divide both sides of the equation for work in terms of charge and potential difference by the time interval. Define power (work done in each unit of time) and current (charge moved in each unit of time) and make appropriate replacements: that will give you a relationship between power, current, and potential difference.

To show these steps, we write $\dfrac{W}{\Delta t} = \dfrac{q}{\Delta t} \times \Delta V$, which can then be expressed as $P = I\Delta V$, where P and I represent **power** and **current**, respectively. The unit of current, the ampere, abbreviated A, is 1 C/s (one coulomb per second).

In space empty of everything except electric charges and their electric fields, particles will be accelerated by electric forces. Inside a wire, even when the wire is a conductor, particles cannot keep on accelerating because they bump into other charged particles. Table 3.2 gives some data that might have been recorded by a scientist in the early days of experiments on electricity. Use this data to determine the relationship between current, voltage, and resistance.

TABLE 4.2 Experimental data for *V*, *R*, and *I*.

Potential difference in V	Resistance (R) in ohms (Ω)	Current in amperes (A)
24	2	12
24	4	6
24	6	4
12	2	6
12	4	3

Experimentally, we find that the current, the charge moving through a uniform wire per second, is proportional to the potential difference we apply to the ends of the wire by a device such as a battery. Current is inversely proportional to the resistance. It has become customary to write the constant of proportion as $\dfrac{1}{R}$ so that the rule is $I = \dfrac{V}{R}$. This is Ohm's law.

We can combine our equation for power with Ohm's law to obtain an equation for **power** in terms of current and resistance:

$$P = IV = I(IR) = I^2R.$$

Note that the equation $P = I^2R$ describes the power that is used to make a current go through a wire or other resistive device. The equation $P = IV$ is more general and can describe situations where some of the power is used to run a motor.

WORKED EXAMPLE 4.2

An air conditioner is hooked up to a 240 V power supply. (Ignore for now the fact that this is alternating current rather than direct current.) It uses a 0.7 A current. The air conditioner cools the air but the motor heats up and has to be air cooled. Don't worry about the numbers for now. Use the bar chart in Figure 4.19 to draw a work-energy bar chart for this process:

Initial energy + Energy supplied = Energy for cooling   + $\Delta U_{\text{int. thermal}}$

FIGURE 4.19 Work-energy bar chart for an air conditioner.

Answer: Here is a possible work-energy bar chart for this process:

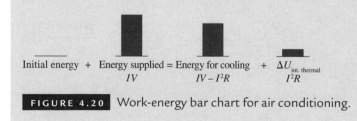

Initial energy + Energy supplied = Energy for cooling   + $\Delta U_{\text{int. thermal}}$
$\qquad\qquad\qquad\quad IV \qquad\qquad\quad IV - I^2R \qquad\qquad I^2R$

FIGURE 4.20 Work-energy bar chart for air conditioning.

This figure also illustrates how the energy supplied electrically cannot all be used for work when there is any kind of dissipative aspect to a system—in this system, some of the energy supplied is lost to thermal energy. You will learn later that the second law of thermodynamics tells us that this must always occur.

Magnetism

Most of the forces we encounter day to day are contact forces. When we push or pull or lift an object, we are in contact with it. With electrical forces we saw that a charged body could attract another charged body and would always attract an uncharged body even though the two bodies were not in contact. Most of you have probably had a chance to play with magnets and have seen that their ends also attract and repel at a distance. Like electricity, magnetism is a long-range force.

How do we know that magnetism is not static electricity? (This is not an easy question, but consider all you know about static electricity from our discussion of that, and think about magnets you have played with. Scientists had to answer this question when research on electricity and magnetism took off seriously in the nineteenth century.)

We can answer this question by describing four observations:

1. If a bar magnet is suspended so that it is free to turn, it rotates and settles down into a position where one end points toward a spot near the geographical north pole and the other end points in the opposite direction. Unmagnetized bodies do not have a preferred orientation even if they have an electric charge on them. The end of the bar that points toward the north is called the "north-seeking" pole of the magnet, or **north pole** for short. The other end is called the "south-seeking" or **south pole**.

2. When two north poles are made to approach one another, they repel. You have felt this if you have ever played with magnets. Two south poles also repel one another, but a north pole of one magnet and a south pole of another magnet attract one another, and "click"

together unless you forcibly hold them apart. If you have any magnets around your house or dorm room, check out the repulsion and attraction for yourself.

3. If you place charges of equal magnitude but opposite sign—one positive, one negative—on two conducting spheres, and then let the spheres touch, the two spheres are then uncharged and neutral. If you pull the north and south poles of two magnets apart after contact, they are still magnetic. That's different from the behavior of electric charges.

4. If you break a magnet in half, each half has a north pole and a south pole. No one has succeeded in producing an isolated north pole or an isolated south pole. If such things existed they would be magnetic charges, but they do not seem to exist.

PICTURE THIS

1. You stack a batch of bar magnets so all the north poles are at one side and all the south poles are at the other side. Is the magnetic field weaker or stronger than the field produced by one bar magnet? Why? (Hint: Think of magnetic field lines going out of the north poles and into the south poles of the magnets.) See Figure 4.21.

2. You place a batch of bar magnets end to end, south pole to north pole as in Figure 4.22, so that there is one south pole at one end and one north pole at the other end. Is the combined magnetic field weaker or stronger than the field produced by one bar magnet? Why?

FIGURE 4.21   Magnets stacked side by side.

FIGURE 4.22   Magnets arranged end to end.

the field is the same as that of one magnet.
magnets end to end, there is just one free north pole and one free south pole, so
duce field lines, so the total field has a greater magnitude. When we connect the
magnet. When we stack magnets side by side, there are more north poles to pro-
each magnet has both a north pole and a south pole, fields start on and end at each
lines. By convention, field lines leave north poles and enter south poles. Because
Answer: 1 and 2. We can think of the magnetic poles as sources of magnetic field

Thermal Physics

If you put something you have just rinsed into a bit of hot oil in a frying pan, you may get spattered by a few drops of hot oil. If you accidentally tip over a pan filled with hot oil onto yourself, you will have to get to a hospital's emergency room. There clearly is a quantitative aspect to thermal physics.

On the other hand, you can pour as much oil from the bottle in the kitchen into your hand as you wish without getting burned. The same substance that can burn can also cool us. Boiling water and ice are examples. There clearly are both qualitative and quantitative aspects to thermal physics.

We call the qualitative aspect **temperature**. We call the quantitative aspect **thermal energy**. ■

✔ QUICK CHECK

Let's see what your current impressions are of temperature and thermal energy:

1. The higher the temperature of a solid body, the more thermal energy it contains.   T F

2. The more of a given substance we have, the more thermal energy it contains at a given temperature.   T F

3. Given equal amounts of the same material, the one at a higher temperature contains more thermal energy than the one at a lower temperature.   T F

4. Equal amounts of different substances at the same temperature may contain different amounts of thermal energy.   T F

5. The greater the difference in temperature between two bodies, the more rapidly thermal energy is transferred from the hotter to the cooler body.   T   F

Answers: These statements are all true.

Temperature is a rough measure of the amount of thermal energy in a given body, but a better definition is that temperature indicates the ability of a body to transfer thermal energy to another body. The more "matter" we have at a given temperature, the more thermal energy it contains. One reason why temperature is not a direct measure of thermal energy in a given body is that the body may be in different states, such as ice and water, but at the same temperature. Water contains more thermal energy than ice at the same temperature.

Now we can look at experiments that demonstrate what we know instinctively.

TEMPERATURE

Every material substance changes in some way when its temperature changes, but those that undergo large enough but continuous enough changes may be used to measure temperature. Because mercury, which is liquid at room temperature, expands significantly as its temperature rises, for quite some time it was used in **thermometers**, devices that measure temperature. Unfortunately, mercury also has a high rate of vaporization and is poisonous, so colored alcohol solutions or substances that change color when the temperature changes are now used for household thermometers. Labs use substances with electrical properties that change when the temperature changes.

Thermometers need to be calibrated. Calibration is accomplished by placing a thermometer in substances that maintain constant temperature and marking the thermometer to indicate its reading at each such temperature. The two main **temperature scales** are those devised by Fahrenheit and Celsius. Temperatures are read in "degrees Fahrenheit" or "degrees Celsius," symbolized by °F or °C, respectively.

✔ **QUICK CHECK**

You may have heard of how these two temperature scales are set.
Let's check:

1. What substance is used to mark 32°F or 0°C on a thermometer?

2. What substance is used to mark 212°F or 100°C on a
   thermometer?

Answers: 1. A mixture of ice and water in equilibrium is at 32°F or 0°C. At that
temperature water starts to freeze if thermal energy is removed or ice to melt if
thermal energy is added. 2. Water boils at sea level at 212°F or 100°C.

THE KELVIN SCALE Thermal energy can be extracted from any body
as long as a body of lower temperature is available. When an object
reaches a temperature at which no thermal energy can be transferred
from it, it's at the lowest possible temperature. This temperature is
called absolute zero or zero Kelvin, written as 0 K. We speak of these
units as kelvins, not degrees Kelvin.

TEMPERATURE CONVERSIONS You probably already know something about temperature conversions. Let's check it out:

✔ **QUICK CHECK**

1. How many degrees Fahrenheit are there between the ice point
   and the boiling point of water?

2. How many degrees Celcius are there between the ice point and
   the boiling point of water?

3. What is the ratio of those degrees Fahrenheit to those
   degrees Celsius?

Answers: 1. We find that 212°F − 32°F = 180 Fahrenheit degrees. (NOT 180°F,
because a temperature difference is not a temperature.) 2. We find that
100°C − 0°C = 100 Celsius degrees. (NOT 100°C.) 3. The ratio of Fahrenheit
to Celsius degrees of the temperature differences between boiling water and
freezing water is $\dfrac{180 \text{ Fahrenheit degrees}}{100 \text{ Celsius degrees}} = \dfrac{9 \text{ F degree}}{5 \text{ C degree}}$.

We can convert from one temperature scale to another using the 9/5 ratio of Fahrenheit to Celsius:

1. Degrees C to degrees F: $T_F = \dfrac{9°F}{5°C} \cdot T_C + 32°F$.

2. Degrees F to degrees C: $T_C = \dfrac{5°C}{9°F} \cdot (T_F - 32 \text{ Fahrenheit degrees})$.

3. Degrees C to degrees K: The Kelvin scale uses degrees of the same size as the Celsius scale, but it sets the lowest possible temperature at 0 K. We then find that 0°C = 273.3 K. Therefore,

$$T_C = T_K + 273.3 \text{ Celsius degrees.}$$
$$T_K = T_C - 273.3 \text{ kelvins.}$$

THERMAL ENERGY

In our current atomic model of matter, we believe that all atoms and molecules in solids, liquids, and gases move randomly, at greater speeds at higher temperatures, and at lower speeds at lower temperatures. The molecules vibrate around fixed positions in solids, move more freely but are still connected to their neighbors in liquids, and move completely freely in gases. In all three, the motions are restricted by bonds to or collisions with neighboring molecules or atoms. That is why the motion is random.

Thus, **thermal energy** is a form of energy where individual parts of a body—molecules within a substance—move differently; the energy is not connected with motion of the body as a whole. When a body with more random energy in its molecules is placed in contact with another body with less random energy in its molecules, the more energetic molecules transfer energy to the less energetic ones and the temperature of the body with more energy decreases while the temperature of the body with less energetic molecules increases. While thermal energy is moving from one body to another we call the *process* **heat transfer**. When you touch a hot dish that has just been removed from the oven, there is a transfer of thermal energy from the pot to your finger. While the energy is moving to your finger there is a heat transfer. We always speak of thermal energy, never of heat as energy, in a body at a constant temperature to emphasize this difference.

Now we can check what you might suspect instinctively:

✔ **QUICK CHECK**

1. Into which of these other forms of energy can thermal energy be converted?

   a. Kinetic energy

   b. Chemical energy

   c. Gravitational potential energy

2. Which of these forms of energy can be converted into thermal energy?

   a. Kinetic energy

   b. Chemical energy

   c. Gravitational potential energy

Answers: 1, 2. a, b, and c.

Thermal energy can be converted into organized energy of motion (kinetic energy), energy stored in chemical bonds (chemical energy), and energy a body has because of its tendency to approach another body while picking up speed in the process (gravitational or electrical potential energy). The steam engine is an example of the first kind, an endothermic chemical reaction illustrates the second, and any process in which an expanding object lifts another object illustrates the third.

THERMODYNAMICS

Thermodynamics studies the interactions between thermal energy, other types of energy, and work done by forces. These interactions are described by the laws of thermodynamics. We'll look at three of them very briefly.

Can a body A at temperature T transfer thermal energy to body B when body B is also at temperature T?

Answer: No. This leads to the **zeroth law of thermodynamics**: When two bodies are in equilibrium—neither one is able to transfer energy to the other—they are at the same temperature. This law was assumed in the discussion of temperature and temperature scales.

Is it possible to create thermal energy out of nothing?

Answer: Your instincts were undoubtedly correct about this. If it were possible to create any kind of energy out of nothing there would not be an energy shortage. (Anyone who advertises a perpetual motion machine is a fraud.) This leads to the **first law of thermodynamics**: The sum of all types of energy within an isolated system remains the same over time; the sum of all types of energy within a system that is not isolated remains the same over time unless energy is provided from or taken away by a body external to the system.

What is a system in thermodynamics? It is similar to a system in mechanics: one or more bodies interacting with one another or being acted upon together by external sources of force and energy over some time period. Part of the art of physics is in selecting one's systems. Good choices—relevant situations to represent a topic of study—make problem solving easier. We will look at that in Chapter 5.

Another statement of the first law of thermodynamics is that energy can neither be created nor destroyed. We can paraphrase that by saying that there is no free lunch.

The **second law of thermodynamics** says that energy can be converted completely from thermal energy to another form only if a body at 0 K is available to act as the body of lower thermal energy. In that case, all the thermal energy can be extracted from a body at a higher temperature in order to do work. Because such a body (at 0 K) is not available in this universe, thermal energy cannot be converted completely into another form of energy, but some must end up in a body at lower temperature, where it is less useful. This says that even if you receive a free lunch, you can't eat it all.

Oscillations

Almost everyone reading this has a yo-yo or something else that can be attached to a string. All you need is something of much greater mass than the string. Hold on to the string and let the mass swing back and forth while your hand remains almost still. Time 10 complete swings back and forth, both for a short length of string and a long length of string.

✔ **QUICK CHECK**

A body swings back and forth in less time when the string is

a) long.   b) short.

Answer: b) short.

The time for one complete swing back and forth is called the period. If you have tried the experiment you have found that the period is less for a short string and greater for a long string. How can this result be used to create a clock?

Any back-and-forth motion that repeats in time is called a **periodic motion**. We say that the moving object oscillates and call it an **oscillator**. A massive object at the end of a light string is a type of oscillator called a **pendulum**. An ideal pendulum—a point mass at the end of a massless string—has a special type of motion called **simple harmonic motion**. If you can find an old-fashioned phonograph that has a turntable that rotates at a constant rate, and can place a small object on the turntable, the shadow of the object on the wall behind it also executes simple harmonic motion, as in Figure 4.23.

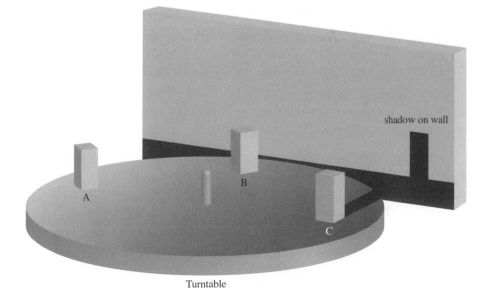

shadow on wall

A

B

C

Turntable

FIGURE 4.23   Shadow in simple harmonic motion of an object in circular motion.

WORKED EXAMPLE 4.3

Describe the movement of the shadow on the wall in Figure 4.23 when the object is at

a) position A.   b) position B.   c) position C.

Answers: a) and c) At the ends, A and C, the object is turning through an arc that is roughly perpendicular to the wall, so its shadow moves slowly. Those are the arcs in Figure 4.24a. b) At position B the arc is now roughly parallel to the wall whether the object is at the front or the back of the turntable, so the shadow moves quickly. Those are the arcs in Figure 4.24b.

a)   b)

FIGURE 4.24   Movement of an object on a turntable at the ends (a) and at the center (b).

You can see that the sort of motion described for the object on the turntable also holds for the pendulum you experimented with. The motion is slow at the ends of the swing and fast at the center.

Look at the motion of your pendulum again. The **period** is the time for one complete back-and-forth motion, but you can get a more accurate value for the period by timing 10 such oscillations and dividing the total time by 10. If you divide the number of complete oscillations by the time, you get the **frequency**—the number of complete oscillations for each unit of time.

PRACTICE

1. Catherine's pendulum goes back and forth in 10 complete oscillations in 4.8 s.
   a) What is its period?
   b) What is its frequency?

2. An object on Marie's turntable goes around in 10 complete circles in 18.0 s.
   a) What is its period?
   b) What is its frequency?

Answers: 1. a) Because the period is the time for one back-and-forth motion of the pendulum, we divide the time for 10 oscillations by 10. The period is 0.48 s. b) The number of oscillations divided by the total time gives the frequency. We can show this as a proportion: $\frac{10}{n_1} = \frac{t_{10}}{1\,s} = f$, where t_{10} is the time for 10 oscillations, n_1 is the number of oscillations in one second, and f is the frequency. Thus, $f = \frac{\text{oscillations}}{\text{s}} = 2.08$ Hz, where 1 Hz (Hertz) equals 1 oscillation per second. 2. a) The period, T, is 1.80 s. b) The frequency is 0.555 Hz.

Finally, draw a graph that shows the oscillation of a pendulum with the vertical axis showing position and the horizontal axis showing time. Remember that the weight, the bob, must stay in about the same place for a longer time at the ends of the motion and change position more quickly when at the center of its motion. Now let's test your instincts again.

WORKED EXAMPLES 4.4

1. How is the frequency related to the period? Use your pendulum and the two previous examples to help you think about this.

   The period T is measured by timing n complete oscillations and dividing the time t by n. The frequency, f, is measured by timing n oscillations and dividing n by t. This gives us $f = \frac{1}{T}$.

2. Does the **amplitude**—half of the distance the pendulum moves in going from one side to the other—depend on the frequency or the period? Again, use your pendulum to help you think about this. What is it that you do that determines the amplitude?

   If the frequency and the period are determined by the length of the string, they are not affected by the amplitude. (This is true as long as the angle of swing from the vertical stays below about 20°.) You can't change the frequency or period by how you move your hand, only the amplitude. A tiny motion produces a small amplitude and a bigger motion produces a bigger amplitude. The amplitude depends on how much energy you provide to the pendulum. This applies to all oscillators.

3. What general shape does your graph have? What have you seen in math that looks like that graph?

   The graph you draw should have a wavelike appearance. It should look like Figure 4.25. The highest points on the graph are the points where the pendulum has the maximum positive displacement from the center. The lowest points are where the pendulum has the maximum negative displacement from the center. (You have to decide which direction of displacement is positive and which is negative.) The horizontal distance between two such high points represents the difference in time between two maximum displacements. The horizontal distance between two such low points also represents the period.

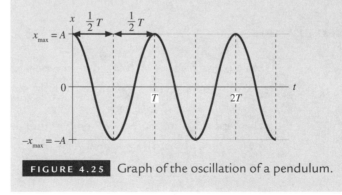

FIGURE 4.25 Graph of the oscillation of a pendulum.

Note that the bob is staying in about the same place when at a crest or a trough, but that position is changing rapidly in time when halfway between a crest or a trough. When we have true simple harmonic motion, the wave shape that results is a **sine wave**. Let's call the displacement of the bob from its center position y and the time t. Then $y = A \cos(\omega t)$ if $x = A$ when $t = 0$, where A is the amplitude and ω is called the **angular frequency**. When you study the mathematical details of this sort of motion in the exercise below you will find that $\omega = 2\pi f$.

TIME TO TRY

Use the fact that $y = A$ both at $t = 0$ and one period later to show that $\omega = 2\pi f$. (You need to know some trigonometry to be able to do this.)

2π radians = 360 degrees.

more useful than degrees when studying waves and oscillations. Remember,

$\omega T = 2\pi$ radians, so $\omega = \dfrac{2\pi}{T} = 2\pi f$. You will find that radian measure is much

Answer: After one period, we have $A = A \cos(\omega T)$. This can hold only if

PICTURE THIS

Run some water in a bathtub, and slosh a sponge up and down at the end of the bathtub. This too is a periodic motion. When you find the correct period the water will slosh up and down in a regular way. The height of these waves varies with the time but the wave crests go up and down in the same places. The number of times per second that the sponge goes up and down or the crests go up and down is the frequency. Half of the vertical distance from a trough, a lowest point, to a crest, a highest point, is the amplitude.

If you take a snapshot of this wave at one instant in time, it is like a graph of vertical position of the water on the vertical axis versus horizontal position in the bathtub on the horizontal axis. This is shown in Figure 4.26. The graph in Figure 4.25 showed the change in displacement from a single central position with time. We can draw such a graph for any point of a wave. Make sure you distinguish it from the picture of the wave in space.

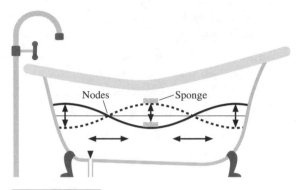

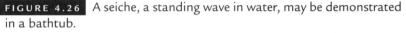

FIGURE 4.26 A seiche, a standing wave in water, may be demonstrated in a bathtub.

We've been looking at objects that move back and forth around one point. When many points are able to move back and forth, such as air molecules bumping into one another, water molecules in the bathtub, or points on a string pulling adjacent points along with them, we get wave shapes. The equation for waves modifies that for oscillations by also including a term that describes a wave shape in space as well as time. Think about how we might modify $y = A \cos(\omega t)$ so that the part that includes time could also include position along a string.

The motion of an oscillator may be described by giving its period or frequency and its amplitude. Because periodic motion occurs in many bodies and systems, along with mechanics it is one of our basic descriptions of nature. ■

Optics

When you stop to think about light and what it might be, you might realize that, with its many different effects, light is very mysterious. Natural philosophers—what scientists were called in ancient and medieval times—could not decide whether an object emitted light or whether light was something emitted by the eye that then returned to the eye. We now know that heating materials so they are very hot produces light. Even in ancient times, people realized that fire and lamps produced light. However, we now also know how to produce light without heating the material. In this section, we'll only be able to look at some of the most obvious, basic observations and their current interpretation.

SHADOWS

WORKED EXAMPLES 4.5

Everyone has seen his or her own shadow. Suppose you turn on a single light bulb and try to stand so that you cast a shadow on a wall.

1. If light is traveling in all directions when it leaves the light bulb, why is there a shadow?

   When light leaves the light bulb, it travels in straight lines. These lines are called **rays**. The rays that your body blocks do not reach the wall and that's why you see a shadow.

2. Why are shadows sometimes very dark and sometimes much less dark?

   When the object is far from the light source, so that the rays are traveling almost parallel to one another, rays traveling toward the position of the shadow are blocked except at the edges of the shadow. When the light source is extended and some rays can reach the shadow because they are not blocked by your body, the shadow is not as clear. Figure 4.27a shows the absence of light at the right when parallel rays strike an arrow-shaped object. Figure 4.27b shows what happens when light rays can reach into the shadow area.

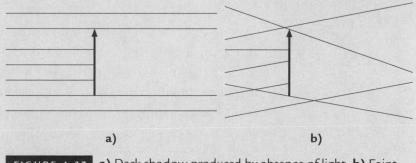

a)   b)

FIGURE 4.27 **a)** Dark shadow produced by absence of light. **b)** Faint shadow produced when some light passes into the region of the shadow.

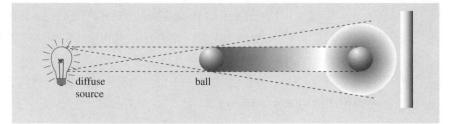

Everyday observations indicate that light travels in straight lines. The sun is very far from the Earth and the rays reaching us are almost, though not perfectly, parallel. Because of this we can use the sun's rays in many experiments where we need parallel rays. An example of this occurs during eclipses of the sun, when the moon obstructs rays from all but a crescent shape of the sun. When the sun's rays go through a small opening the figure seen is a crescent. If the rays traveled in all directions we would just see a blur.

What does travel in straight lines tell us about the nature of light? Keep this question in mind as you read the following sections.

DIFFRACTION

Let's talk about sound waves for a minute. Do you have to be in a direct line with a person who is talking to hear that person's voice? The answer is no, because sound waves bend around obstacles the way that water waves bend around pilings at a pier. Waves in a liquid or solid medium can change direction at openings and obstacles.

TIME TO TRY

Carefully take a single-edge razor blade and make a straight cut about one inch long in an index card. Hold the cut—our technical name for such a narrow opening is a slit— vertically in front of one eye. Close the other eye and look at a light bulb from a distance. Be sure all other bulbs are turned off. A street lamp works well for this. You should see light coming directly through the slit, but also see a band of light on either side of the slit. There will be a pattern there with some vertical dark lines intersecting the bright areas. A schematic drawing of the pattern should look something like Figure 4.28. A picture of an actual pattern is shown in Figure 4.29.

FIGURE 4.28 Pattern seen in diffraction of light through a single slit.

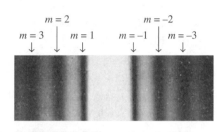

$m = 3$ $m = 2$ $m = 1$ $m = -1$ $m = -2$ $m = -3$

FIGURE 4.29 A diffraction pattern produced by a single wavelength of light.

The darkest band in Figure 4.28 shows where your eye sees the most light and the lightest band shows where your eye sees the least light in the single-slit **diffraction pattern**. What do these diffraction patterns tell you about light?

Answer: The patterns show that light has bent when going through the slit in the same way that sound waves bend when going through a door. This indicates that light has wave properties. The pattern will be clearest if you look at a sodium lamp street light, because there is one predominant color in the light. If you look at an incandescent bulb you will have the same pattern in many different colors but spread out to differing extents. In class, you will learn how to represent this same information with a graph of intensity versus horizontal position for such a picture on a screen.

COLOR

When you listen to music you hear many different pitches. Pitch describes how low or high a particular tone sounds. It turns out that pitch is the brain's subjective interpretation of frequency, and volume is its subjective interpretation of amplitude (technically, amplitude squared). Color is the brain's subjective interpretation of frequency, and brightness is its subjective interpretation of amplitude. You see many different overlapping patterns when you look at a white light, because white contains all frequencies of visible light. The different frequencies bend through different angles when going through a slit.

WHAT IS LIGHT?

How can you interpret the existence of shadows and diffraction? Can you reconcile the different ideas?

Answer: Water waves bend around pilings, but when you look at waves in the ocean or in a large lake, you see that they pretty much travel in straight lines. Although Newton used a particle model for light, physicists had to change their ideas after early-nineteenth-century experiments showed diffraction and also indicated that light from two different slits could interfere to make different patterns from those produced by diffraction from one slit alone. When we can ignore the bending and look at rays of light, we say that we are dealing with geometrical optics. We only have to look at the straight lines along which the light waves travel. When we have to consider bending and recombining of light waves, we say that we are using the physical optics model of light.

You may have heard of photons. When light is absorbed by certain metals, and electrons are ejected, there is a minimum amount of light energy that must be absorbed for this to occur. This quantum of light energy is called a **photon**. A photon acts like a particle of light. Quantum mechanics has now shown that light can act both as a particle and as a wave, but not simultaneously. If you take up quantum mechanics in your physics course, your instructor will have time to go into this.

Atomic and Nuclear Physics

Even as late as the nineteenth century, a scientist as good as Ernst Mach, whose musings on the origin of mass contributed to Einstein's work, could claim that there was no evidence for the existence of atoms. By 1900, however, radioactivity, the electron, and quantum physics had been discovered.

Pure gold is soft and can be beaten down to incredible thinness to form gold foil. Cut the foil in half, and then cut that in half, and keep on going. How many such cuts can you make and still have gold? We now know that each gold atom has a diameter of about 3×10^{-10} cm, but it took a combination of theory and experiment to show that the atomic hypothesis was correct.

You probably have absorbed some ideas about atoms. Let's check:

✔ **QUICK CHECK**

(True or False)

1. An atom is the basic unit of matter and cannot be subdivided further.   T F

2. An atom is composed of a massive positively charged nucleus and very low-mass electrons.   T F

3. The size of an atom is determined by the size of the nucleus.   T F

4. The size of an atom is determined by the range of its electrons.   T F

5. The nucleus of an atom is made up of positively charged protons and negatively charged electrons.   T F

6. The nucleus of an atom is made up of positively charged protons and neutral particles called neutrons.   T F

7. The electrons in an atom are organized into shells with those of lowest energy closest to the nucleus.   T F

8. It's easy to remove electrons from completely filled shells, as is the case in the noble gases helium, neon, argon, and krypton.   T F

9. All nuclei are always stable and never change.   T F

10. Radioactive nuclei can emit electrons, gamma rays, and helium nuclei (alpha particles).   T F

Answers: 1. False. By providing energy we can eject electrons from atoms. The existence of radioactivity shows that nuclei are not all stable. 2. True. 3. False. Electrons are distributed outside the nucleus in what is sometimes described as an "electron cloud." This electron cloud is of the order of 100,000 or 10^5 times larger than the nucleus. 4. True. (See answer 3.) 5. False. This is a subtle quantum effect, but electrons confined to a region the size of the nucleus would have to have preposterously high velocities and kinetic energies. 6. True. This has been verified by many experiments. 7. True. On average, this is true, although the angular momentum of the electrons also determines their distribution. 8. False. The ionization energy, the energy needed to remove an electron from a filled shell, is very high. That's partly why the noble gases don't react chemically. 9. False. If that were so, there would be no radioactivity. 10. True.

Your physics course will introduce atomic theory after covering older topics such as mechanics, thermodynamics, electromagnetism, waves and optics, and a brief introduction to quantum physics. If there is time it will also cover the properties of atomic nuclei and the basics of radioactivity. Rarely will your course have time to cover some of the most fascinating topics: the smallest particles known—those which make up the proton and the neutron and other newly discovered particles—and cosmology, what is known about the universe as a whole.

Final Stretch!

Now that you have finished reading this chapter it is time to stretch your brain and check how much you have learned.

RUNNING WORDS

Here are the terms introduced in this chapter. Write them in a notebook and define them in your own words. Then go back through the chapter to check on their meanings, and on any formulas associated with them. Make corrections as needed and try to list examples of the use of each term.

Electric charge, positive charge, negative charge

Coulomb's law

Charge polarization and induction

Electric field and electric field lines

Electric potential energy, electric potential and potential difference

Insulators and Conductors

Ohm's law and electric power, current and resistance

Magnetic poles

Temperature, thermometers, and temperature scales

Temperature conversions

Thermal energy

The laws of thermodynamics

Periodic motion

Oscillation, period, frequency, and amplitude

Light rays and shadows

Diffraction, photons

Structure of an atom and its nucleus

WEB RESOURCES

For additional help, enter any of the topics listed in "What Did You Learn?" or boldface section titles in Google or another search engine. Again, Wikipedia will give you a very high level overview, so you should look for sites at an appropriate level.

> ■ *Several of the Phet simulations—Balloons and Static Electricity, John Travoltage, and Electric Field Hockey—will help illustrate electric field concepts. Try some other topics on that site as well.*
>
> **http://phet.colorado.edu/get_phet/index.php**

5 Solving Problems

When you complete this chapter, you should be able to:

■ Choose the best physical system for the solution of a problem.

■ Choose the best model to apply to that system.

■ Choose among physical and mathematical representations to solve that problem.

■ Check your results to see if they make sense.

■ Apply estimates both at the beginning and at the end of problem-solving.

■ Know how to answer conceptual multiple choice questions.

Systems, Models, Representations, and Strategies

When you solve physics problems several bodies may be interacting, but only some of them may undergo significant changes. For instance, when a ball is thrown up in the air or to another person, the people throw and catch the ball, but do not otherwise enter into the problem. It may be possible to treat the Earth as a source of a gravitational force, but otherwise ignore it. In this example, the ball is the system, and the force description or model of nature was used. In addition, you may draw a pictorial representation of the ball traversing its path, then represent the ball as a point particle and turn the pictorial representation into a diagrammatic representation by adding coordinate axes and known information, and finally use these representations to write a mathematical representation of the given problem. These choices represent one strategy for solving a problem about a ball in the air.

In another way of solving the same problem, you might treat the ball and the Earth as a system while still ignoring the people who throw and catch the ball. Then you would find that, by eliminating one step in the mathematical process, the energy model gives you a simpler mathematical representation. You would then solve for velocities directly, but would not have information about forces.

How do you choose a system and the best model when given a problem in school, or in real life? The answer lies in following a strategy of problem-solving:

1. Read the problem and then state it in your own words.

   That is the verbal representation.

2. Make notes listing known quantities and, when possible, what the unknown quantities are. You might have to return to this step after constructing several additional representations of the problem.

3. Construct a pictorial representation. Until you are very skilled at drawing diagrams do not omit this step.

4. Construct a diagrammatic representation. ALWAYS include coordinate axes and their scale. Add the list of known and unknown quantities to this diagram. For instance, positions at particular times should be indicated on the diagram with the values of position and time written in.

5. Use the diagram and the information in it to decide what the system should be and what model you will use. If you are solving problems at the end of a chapter, the model may be clear and only the system must be chosen. However, if you are studying for a final exam, you should try to find a mixed set of problems so you can practice choosing the easiest model to solve.

6. Now write down the mathematical representation in symbols. For example, for the trajectory of a ball you might choose among the following equations for the force model:

$$a_x = 0$$
$$a_y = -g$$
$$v_x = v_{0,x}$$
$$v_y = v_{0,y} - gt$$
$$x = x_0 + v_{0,x}t$$
$$y = y_0 + v_{0,y}t - \frac{1}{2}gt^2$$

Usually not all of them will be needed to solve any one problem.

On the other hand, if you don't need information about the accelerations, you could use the energy model and write the following:

$$\frac{1}{2}m(v_{x,i}^2 + v_{y,i}^2) + mgy_i = \frac{1}{2}m(v_{x,f}^2 + v_{y,f}^2) + mgy_f.$$

7. Solve the equation or equations for the unknown quantity or quantities, and then substitute in numerical values.

8. Look at your answers. If a baseball is traveling at $0.000081 \ \frac{m}{s}$ or faster than $50 \ \frac{m}{s}$, it is either being carried by a mass of ants or was shot from a cannon, because $45 \ \frac{m}{s}$ equals 100 miles per hour. When the physical situation is too abstract, instinct may not help, but you will usually be able to assess your responses if you have time to think about them. Practice this when doing homework, and it will become instinctive on exams.

Every textbook has a list of steps similar to this in it. It seems tedious. Students generally prefer to memorize the solutions to a limited number of problems, hoping that problems on exams will be similar enough to those. But one problem that involves a roller coaster may need the force model while another one may need the energy model. If you use the wrong model, you're sunk on an exam. This chapter will help you practice problem-solving strategy so that you will be on the right track when taking the next physics course.

✔ **QUICK CHECK**

State whether each of the following items describes a system, a model, a representation, or possibly more than one. Trust your instincts.

1. Two cars collide at an intersection.

2. The pressure at the base of a column of liquid is directly proportional to the height of the column.

3. A high energy proton bombards a uranium nucleus. What is the closest distance of approach if the proton has a 10 MeV energy?

4. $$\begin{cases} ma_x = F_x. \\ F_x = \dfrac{1}{4\pi\epsilon_0}\dfrac{q_1 q_2}{x^2}. \end{cases}$$

5.

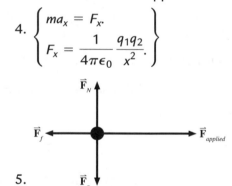

6.

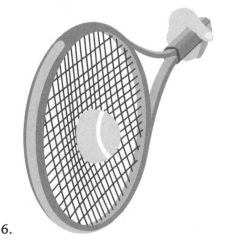

7. Fifty gm of water at 80°C is mixed with 100 gm of water at 35°C. What is the final temperature of the mixture when it reaches equilibrium?

8. $m_1 c_W T_{1,i} + m_2 c_W T_{2,i} = (m_1 + m_2) c_W T_f.$

9. A ray of light from a lamp in the side of a swimming pool makes an angle of 30° with the surface of the water. At what angle to the surface of the water does the refracted ray exit the pool?

10.

Answers: 1. This is a description of a system of two cars that interact. 2. This is a model because it describes how the height affects the pressure at the bottom. It also contains the mathematical representation in words. 3. This is a verbal representation of a problem. It also implies that the nucleus and the proton will be the system. 4. This is a mathematical representation of the acceleration of charge 2 at position x when charge 1, fixed at x = 0, exerts the force shown on it. 5. This is a diagrammatic representation because the body has been reduced to a point and forces on it are shown by vector arrows. 6. This is a pictorial representation. You can turn it into a diagrammatic representation by changing the ball to a point and showing the forces on it by vector arrows. 7. This is a verbal representation. It also tells you what your system is. 8. This is a mathematical representation of the solution to the problem stated in question 7. 9. This is a verbal representation. It also tells you that your system consists of the ray of light and the surface of the pool. 10. This is a pictorial representation of a locomotive pulling a train. We don't have enough information to determine what the system will be, or what is known or unknown.

Systems

Remember that we looked at many different models of physical systems in Chapters 3 and 4. We had mechanical models; the thermal model, itself an extension of the energy picture; the wave model; two different optic models; and we touched on modern quantum physics and nuclear models as well. Let's look at a few examples where we only want to determine what the system is.

PICTURE THIS

1. A couple of teenagers on roller blades skate directly toward one another. We want to know where they will meet. They are on a driveway, and there is a hedge on either side of the driveway. Two other teenagers are observing them. What, and whom, should we include in our system?

2. A couple of teenagers on roller blades skate directly toward one another. We want to know how much thermal energy will result from their collision. They are on a driveway, and there is a hedge on either side of the driveway. Two other teenagers are observing them. What, and whom, should we include in our system?

3. A "Rube Goldberg" device operates so that a ball rolls down an incline and strikes the upper part of a hinged lever so the longer bottom part of the lever knocks over a can of soda. That pulls a string, which releases another ball that rolls down another incline and hits a switch that activates a motor to open a door that lets the dog out into the yard. What is the "system" here for physical analysis? Is there only one?

4. A scientific monitor at a nuclear power station has a Geiger counter to measure radiation levels. She can take data at various positions outside the reactor core. There is also a temporary holding pool for spent fuel rods at one side of the reactor core. She wants to check on whether or not the readings on the gauges in the control room are accurate. Those gauges are supposed to give separate reactor and holding pool radiation levels. What should she take as a system and where should she make measurements of radiation levels?

5. A teenager wants to construct his own telescope. He knows he needs cardboard tubes and two lenses. What is (are) his system(s) after he decides what sorts of lenses he needs to buy?

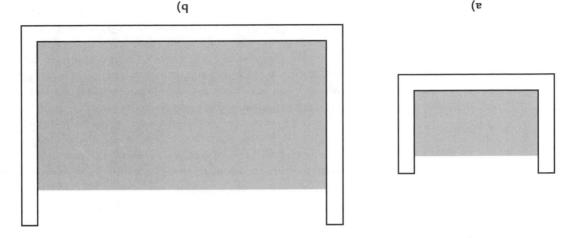

b)

a)

FIGURE 5.1 a) The holding pool. b) The reactor, seen in cross section, core not shown.

Answers: 1. Each of the two teenagers is a system. If we know their initial positions and velocities, we can determine where they will meet, as long as they are on a level surface. If the driveway is on an incline, we will still use each teenager as a system, but determine his or her acceleration by regarding the driveway and the Earth as sources of external forces. (Sources of external forces are not part of the system because they are external to the system.) In the latter case, the equations are a bit more complicated but can still be solved. (We need to recognize that the two teenagers are both at the same position when they meet.) 2. Now the system consists of both teenagers, the driveway, and the Earth. The teenagers' initial kinetic energy ends up as thermal energy if the driveway is level and they come to a stop. If the driveway is not level, some gravitational potential energy will end up as thermal energy or kinetic energy, depending on the relative masses of the two teenagers and whether or not they come to a complete stop. 3. We have to break this up into a series of interactions. We have different objects interacting in each step, so we have a different system for each step. We first find the velocity of the ball at the bottom of the incline. If we use the force model, the ball is the system. If we use the energy model, the system includes the ball and Earth, but the incline only acts as a constraint if we can ignore friction. The second system consists of the ball, the hinged lever, and the soda can. If the string's mass can be ignored, the energy ends up as thermal energy for the most part with only a little bit given to the string. The switch also uses a small portion of the second ball's kinetic energy. If we treat the wall holding the switch as immobile, the second ball's kinetic energy also ends up as thermal energy. Our analysis stops here, because the motor, being electric, requires a model that includes magnetic forces on current carrying wires. 4. If any significant quantity of radiation leaves the holding pool, it cannot be ignored. Therefore, the system has two radiation sources—the reactor and the pool. Let's assume the reactor is cylindrical and the pool is rectangular. They are pictured from the side in Figure 5.1:

It seems likely that the radiation would be most intense between the reactor and the pool, of medium intensity to the left of the pool, and that the intensity would fall off more rapidly with distance to the right of the reactor than to its left, although that depends on the size of the pool and how much radioactive material it holds. She would also expect medium readings in front of and behind the reactor. Therefore, she should take readings all around the cylindrical reactor in circles of different radii. 5. The teenager could construct his telescope experimentally by holding one lens in front of his eye and then finding the position where the second lens works best. He might need a friend's help, both in holding the second lens and in measuring the distance between the two lenses, although he could also use clay to hold the bottoms of the lenses. However, if he wants to know what lenses to buy, he will need to know the effective focal length of the human eye, so it too might be considered a part of the system.

Your Starting Point: How Do You Begin?

WORKED EXAMPLE 5.1

> A professional baseball player, a pitcher, throws a ball straight up in the air.
>
> Most textbook problems will deal only with the ball while it is in the air. However, we can learn a lot about systems and models if we include the acts of throwing and catching the ball in our example.
>
> 1. We will take the ball as the system in each case but look separately at
>
>   a. the ball at rest in the hand.
>
>   b. the ball being thrown while it has not yet left the hand.
>
>   c. the ball after it has left the hand and is in the air. (Why aren't the cases of the ball rising and the ball falling two different systems?)

    d. the ball being caught but not yet having stopped moving.

    e. the ball at rest in the hand. [This is identical to (a) but occurs at a later time.]

2. For each of these, the force model can be used to list which bodies interact with and exert forces on our system, the ball. In addition, you can state whether the sum of forces on the ball is zero, positive, or negative. Take the upward direction as positive. A quick sketch—a pictorial representation of the ball and the bodies interacting with it—may help you follow the reasoning shown.

Answers: Here are the interactions:

    a. Hand on ball, up; Earth on ball, down. Sum is zero.

    b. Hand on ball, up; Earth on ball, down. Sum is positive because the hand is exerting a greater upward force than the Earth's downward force.

    c. Earth on ball, down. Negative.

    d. Hand on ball, up; Earth on ball, down. Sum is positive because the hand is exerting a greater upward force than the Earth's downward force.

    e. Hand on ball, up; Earth on ball, down. Sum is zero.

Note how many assumptions we make. We treat the ball as a point particle, ignore air resistance, the force the ball exerts on the hand, the force the ball exerts on the Earth, buoyancy, and any possible rotational motion on the ball.

Always look for all the unstated assumptions in any problem. They help you simplify the problem. ■

3. For each of these you can draw a free-body diagram. It will show the ball as a point, with the forces on it shown by vector arrows. This is your diagrammatic representation. If you had trouble with part 2, you may want to draw the diagrams first. They are shown next.

Answers:

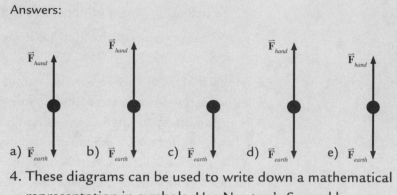

a) $\vec{F}_{earth}$ b) $\vec{F}_{earth}$ c) $\vec{F}_{earth}$ d) $\vec{F}_{earth}$ e) $\vec{F}_{earth}$

4. These diagrams can be used to write down a mathematical representation in symbols. Use Newton's Second law, $a_y = \dfrac{\sum F_y^{external}}{m}$, with a vertical coordinate axis, called the y-axis, directed vertically upward. (You might want to go back and add a y-axis to each diagram.)

Answers:

a. $\vec{F}_{\text{hand on ball}} + \vec{F}_{\text{Earth on ball}} = 0$ by Newton's First law. (If there is no change in velocity—here velocity is zero—then the sum of the forces on an object must be zero.) In terms of components along the y-axis, $F_{\text{hand on ball}} - F_{\text{Earth on ball}} = 0$.

b. $m\vec{a} = \vec{F}_{\text{hand on ball}} + \vec{F}_{\text{Earth on ball}}$ or $ma_y = F_{\text{hand on ball}} - F_{\text{Earth on ball}} > 0$, because the hand is exerting a greater force upward than the force the Earth is exerting downward. (Otherwise the ball would not accelerate upward.)

c. Here, $m\vec{a} = \vec{F}_{\text{Earth on ball}}$ or $ma_y = -F_{\text{Earth on ball}}$.

d. $m\vec{a} = \vec{F}_{\text{hand on ball}} + \vec{F}_{\text{Earth on ball}}$ or $ma_y = F_{\text{hand on ball}} - F_{\text{Earth on ball}} > 0$, because the hand is exerting a greater force upward than the force the Earth is exerting downward. (The $\sum \vec{F}^{ext} > 0$, because the hand is slowing the ball down.)

e. $\vec{F}_{\text{hand on ball}} + \vec{F}_{\text{Earth on ball}} = 0$ by Newton's First law. (If there is no change in velocity—here velocity is zero—then the sum of the forces on an object must be zero.) In terms of components along the y-axis, $F_{\text{hand on ball}} - F_{\text{Earth on ball}} = 0$.

When you write Newton's Second law as a vector equation you add all forces, because the directions are included in the vector symbols. When you write the law in terms of components you must take care to choose the correct sign for each component. ■

Alternate Model: **The Energy Model**

WORKED EXAMPLE 5.2

If you do not need to know the acceleration or the time, then the energy model may be quicker and easier. Let's write down the sum of energies for each state of the ball:

a. The ball at rest in the hand

b. The ball being thrown while it has not yet left the hand

c. The ball after it has left the hand and is in the air (Why aren't the cases of the ball rising and the ball falling two different systems?)

d. The ball being caught but not yet having stopped moving

e. The ball at rest in the hand [This is identical to (a) but occurs at a later time.]

Remember that Earth must be included in our system along with the ball when we use the energy model. Gravity is not considered a separate external force, because it is taken into account in the gravitational potential energy. For each system, write down the formula for the kinetic energy, the gravitational potential energy, and the total energy of the ball–Earth system.

In order to solve this, we will first use a diagram method and then use these work-energy bar charts to write down the energies. Review Work-Energy Bar Charts in Chapter 3. A complete diagram includes bars for initial and final states of the system, but in the following bar charts only the individual states will be shown.

BAR CHARTS

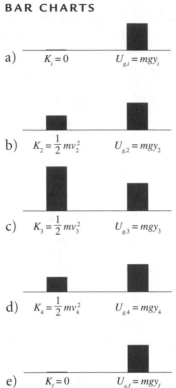

a) $K_i = 0$ $U_{g,i} = mgy_i$

b) $K_2 = \dfrac{1}{2}mv_2^2$ $U_{g,2} = mgy_2$

c) $K_3 = \dfrac{1}{2}mv_3^2$ $U_{g,3} = mgy_3$

d) $K_4 = \dfrac{1}{2}mv_4^2$ $U_{g,4} = mgy_4$

e) $K_f = 0$ $U_{g,f} = mgy_f$

MATHEMATICAL REPRESENTATIONS IN THE ENERGY MODEL

You can now use the bar charts to write down the expressions for the types of energy you have.

a. $K_i = 0;\ U_{g,i} = mgy_i;\ E_i = K_i + U_{g,i} = mgy_i.$

b. Both the gravitational potential energy and the kinetic energy increase as the ball travels upward.

$$K_2 = \frac{1}{2}mv_2^2;\ U_{g,2} = mgy_2;\ E_2 = \frac{1}{2}mv_2^2 + mgy_2.$$

These formulas hold true at every instant as the ball is thrown. In a problem we would usually want to insert the values at the instant when the ball leaves the hand. Note that we can ignore the force the hand applies if we know the ball's velocity.

c. Here, $K_3 = \frac{1}{2}mv_3^2;\ U_{g,3} = mgy_3;\ E_3 = \frac{1}{2}mv_3^2 + mgy_3.$

This is correct for each instant when the ball is in the air

When the ball is at the highest point, its energy is all potential. Because it goes from moving up, v positive, to moving down, v negative, relative to the coordinate axis we have chosen, its velocity must be zero at the highest point and at that point and time only. The ball slows down and reverses direction, but it does not "hover." It is at the highest point for no length of time at all.

Because all of the ball's energy is potential at the highest point, h_{top}, its gravitational potential energy at that point is equal to the kinetic energy it had when it left the hand with velocity v_{hand}. We can write

$$mgh_{top} = \frac{1}{2}mv_{hand}^2,$$

and find h_{top} if we know v_{hand}, where $h_{top} = y_3 - y_i$.

d. Both the gravitational potential energy and the kinetic energy decrease as the ball is caught.

$$K_4 = \frac{1}{2}mv_4^2; \; U_{g,4} = mgy_4; \; E_4 = \frac{1}{2}mv_4^2 + mgy_4.$$

These formulas hold true at every instant as the ball is caught. In a problem we would usually want to insert the values at the instant when the ball reaches the hand. If the ball is caught at the same height at which it left the hand, it reaches the hand with the same speed it had when it left the hand.

e. This is the same as the answer to (a) when the ball is back at the 1.20 m height: $K = 0$; $U_{g,f} = mgy_f$; $E_f = K_f + U_{g,f} = mgy_f$.

If you have values for enough heights and velocities, you can now solve for those that are unknown. Most textbooks will only ask you to use one or two parts of this example.

When using the energy model, prepare a bar chart with a bar for each type of energy at the initial time, and a bar for each type of energy at the later time. Leave a space for a bar for work done by a body that was not included in your system and one for any thermal internal energy at the end. ∎

TIME TO TRY

Be sure to think about your strategy. Which model will be simplest to work with? What do pictorial and diagrammatic representations suggest you use for the mathematical representation?

1. A 50 gm ball leaves a hand at a speed of $30 \, \frac{m}{s}$ at a point 1.6 m above the ground. How far above the ground is the highest point the ball reaches?

2. A 50 gm ball is dropped from a dorm window that is 18.0 m above the ground. What is its speed just before if strikes the ground?

3. A 50 gm ball leaves a hand at a speed of $30 \, \frac{m}{s}$ at a point 1.6 m above the ground. How long does it take the ball to reach the highest point?

4. A 50 gm ball leaves a hand at a speed of $30 \, \frac{m}{s}$ at a point 1.6 m above the ground. How long does it take the ball to return to the hand that threw it?

Answers: 1. This is case (c) under Your Starting Point, at the instant when the ball has just left the hand and at the instant when it reaches the highest point. Use the energy model because you don't need time or acceleration. Remember that the velocity is zero at the highest point. Because total mechanical energy remains constant, set $E_i = E_f$, or $\frac{1}{2}mv_i^2 + mgh_i = \frac{1}{2}mv_f^2 + mgh_f$. Then, $h_f = 47.5$ m. **2.** Use the energy model and the same equation as in (1). Note that the initial velocity is zero for a body that is "dropped." $v_f = 18.8 \, \frac{m}{s}$. **3.** Here we must use a force model, but we already know the acceleration produced by gravity. We therefore apply a kinematics model and use $v_f = v_0 - gt = 0$, so $t = 3.06$ s. **4.** This problem is solved most easily by combining the energy and kinematics models. Use $\frac{1}{2}mv_i^2 + mgh_i = \frac{1}{2}mv_f^2 + mgh_f$ and note that the initial and final heights are equal. Therefore, the final speed is the same as the initial speed, although the velocity has a different direction. So, you can solve $v_f = -v_0 = v_0 - gt$ to find $t = 6.12$ s. When there is no air resistance it takes the same amount of time for a ball to fall from the highest point as it took it to rise to the highest point.

Momentum: **A Conservation Law for the Force Model**

The total energy of a system does not change unless work is done on the system by a body that has been chosen to be outside the system. Energy can end up as internal thermal energy, so we cannot always know the kinetic and gravitational or electrostatic potential energies of a system at both initial and final times.

There is a conservation law without this drawback. Define the **momentum** of a body as $\vec{p} = m\vec{v}$. Add the momenta of all bodies in your system at a given time. Then the sum of the momenta of all those bodies at a later time has exactly the same value without any exceptions if no external force acts on the system. For two bodies, we can write $\vec{p}_{1,i} + \vec{p}_{2,i} = \vec{p}_{1,f} + \vec{p}_{2,f}$. This law is very useful in collision problems.

When an external force $\vec{F}$ acts on a single body that initially has momentum $\vec{p}_i = m\vec{v}_i$ for a time interval Δt, then $\vec{p}_i + \vec{F}\Delta t = \vec{p}_f$. The quantity $\vec{F}\Delta t$ is the **impulse** imparted to the body by the force. If we know the initial and final velocities of a body of mass m, then the impulse has been $\vec{F}\Delta t = \vec{p}_f - \vec{p}_i$. In either of its versions in this paragraph, this law is known as the momentum-impulse theorem. The conventional symbol for impulse is $\vec{J}$.

The example of the ball is a good system for illustrating how we define the momentum of the ball and for how we can combine initial and final momenta to determine impulses.

WORKED EXAMPLES 5.3

Let's look at some specific examples.

1. A girl throws a handball at the wall of a court as hard as she can. It strikes the wall head-on at a speed of 30 $\frac{m}{s}$ at a point 1.2 m above the ground and leaves the wall perpendicular to the wall at a speed of 15 $\frac{m}{s}$. What impulse did the wall give to the ball?

2. If the ball is in contact with the wall for 0.10 s, how large a force did the ball exert on the wall?

3. As a result of drunk driving, two cars collide head-on at night. The 1,500 kg car is headed due east at 40 $\frac{m}{s}$. The 1,200 kg car is headed due west at 35 $\frac{m}{s}$. The cars stick together after colliding. What is the velocity of the two cars after the collision?

Answers:

1. First we draw a sketch of the ball approaching, striking, and receding from the wall, as in Figure 5.2.

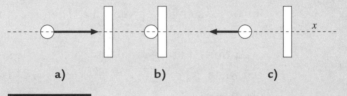

FIGURE 5.2   A ball **a)** approaching, **b)** striking, and **c)** leaving a wall.

Because this is a collision problem, it suggests that you solve the problem by using the equation $\vec{F}\Delta t = \vec{p}_f - \vec{p}_i$ in one dimension. If you pick an x-axis directed to the right, you can write $F\Delta t = p_f - p_i = mv_f - mv_i = 30 \text{ gm}(-15 \text{ m/s} - 30 \text{ m/s}) = -1{,}350 \frac{\text{kg} \cdot \text{m}}{\text{s}}$.

Note that there is no special unit for momentum, just the product of the units for mass and velocity. Convince yourself that all the signs are correct relative to the x-axis's direction.

2. Because you already know the impulse, J, the force is

$$F = \frac{J}{\Delta t} = \frac{-1{,}350 \frac{\text{kg} \cdot \text{m}}{\text{s}}}{0.10 \text{ s}} = -13{,}500 \text{ N.}$$

3. What strategy should you follow? Use your instinct. In what direction will the combined cars move after colliding? Which car has the greater momentum before the collision? Are the momenta of the two cars in the same direction before the collision? Do the two momenta have the same signs when you put a coordinate axis in the problem?

Start with a pictorial representation, as in Figure 5.3. You probably will not need to go to a point particle diagram for this problem. You can then go straight to the mathematical representation.

FIGURE 5.3 Cars headed toward a collision.

Here you can use the fact that the total momentum after the collision is equal to the total momentum before the collision: $\vec{p}_{1,i} + \vec{p}_{2,i} = \vec{P}_{total,f}$

or $m_1v_1 + m_2v_2 = (m_1 + m_2)v_f$ and $v_f = \dfrac{m_1v_1 + m_2v_2}{(m_1 + m_2)} =$

$\dfrac{(1{,}500 \text{ kg})(40 \text{ m/s}) - (1{,}200 \text{ kg})(35 \text{ m/s})}{2{,}700 \text{ kg}} = 6.7 \dfrac{m}{s}.$

Here our instinct that the greater overcomes the lesser holds true; the net momentum after the collision is east, in the direction of the car that originally had the greater momentum. If this agreed with your prediction, you could have used it for a check on the accuracy of your calculation.

TIME TO TRY

1. A 60 kg skater heading north at $10 \dfrac{m}{s}$ collides with a 50 kg skater heading due south at $12 \dfrac{m}{s}$. They clutch one another as they collide. What is their total momentum just before and just after the collision?

2. The skaters think that this is so much fun that they collide again. This time the 60 kg skater is headed south at $8 \dfrac{m}{s}$ and the 50 kg skater is headed north at $12 \dfrac{m}{s}$.
   a) What is their total momentum just before and just after the collision?
   b) What is their (joint) velocity right after the collision?

3. A 52 g ball is headed due east at $40 \dfrac{m}{s}$ at the moment a bat strikes it. It leaves the bat headed due west at $45 \dfrac{m}{s}$.
   a) What was the change of momentum of the ball?
   b) If the bat was in contact with the ball for 0.12 s, what force, magnitude and direction, did the bat exert on the ball?

Answers 1. Choose north as the positive direction. The total momentum is zero because one skater has momentum $+600 \frac{kg \cdot m}{s}$ and the other has momentum $-600 \frac{kg \cdot m}{s}$. The total momentum remains the same for an isolated system. (Forces the skaters exert on one another are internal forces. Internal forces do not change the momentum of a system.) 2. a) The total momentum is

$$+600 \frac{kg \cdot m}{s} - 480 \frac{kg \cdot m}{s} = +120 \frac{kg \cdot m}{s}.$$

b) It is

$$\frac{120 \frac{kg \cdot m}{s}}{110 \, kg} = 1.09 \frac{m}{s}.$$

3. a) Take west as the positive direction, because our standard definition of the change in a quantity is the final value minus the initial value. Then,

$$\Delta \vec{p} = 2.34 \frac{kg \cdot m}{s} - \left(-2.08 \frac{kg \cdot m}{s}\right) = 4.42 \frac{kg \cdot m}{s}.$$

b) Because $\Delta \vec{p} = \vec{F} \Delta t$,

$$\vec{F} = +36.8 \, N = 36.8 \, N, W.$$

Sample More Complex Standard Physics Problem

A train traveling on a straight track takes off from a station at exactly 12:15 PM. It arrives at the next station and comes to a stop exactly 8.00 minutes later. If the train travels at its maximum acceleration for each half of the trip, what was the magnitude of the acceleration? Assume the distance between stops is 19,200 m.

1. How do you begin solving the problem?

2. List all known and unknown information in the problem.

3. Prepare a schematic list of the information in question 2.

4. If it is possible, draw a sketch and turn it into a diagram.

5. What unknown quantities must we find?

Answers:

1. You read the problem carefully and look for cues that might indicate what strategy would help solve the problem.

2. We note what is given: The travel time is 8.00 minutes, the total distance traveled is 19,200 m, the train never travels at constant velocity, and the train's speed increases for half the time and decreases for half the time. Because the acceleration has its maximum value when positive and when negative, each half of the trip must take the same amount of time.

3. We'll take $t_i = 0$. We'll call the halfway time t_1 and the end of the trip t_2. We'll call the initial position $x_i = 0$, the halfway point x_1, and the end point x_2. Now we can prepare a summary in a tabular form:

$t_i = 0$ $t_1 = 4.00 \text{ min} = 240 \text{ s}$ $t_2 = 8.00 \text{ min} = 480 \text{ s}$

$x_i = 0$ $x_1 = 9{,}600 \text{ m}$ $x_2 = 19{,}200 \text{ m}$

$v_i = 0$ $v_1 = ?$ $v_2 = 0$

$\qquad\quad a_1 = ?$ $\qquad a_2 = ?$

4. (a) Sketch (pictorial representation):

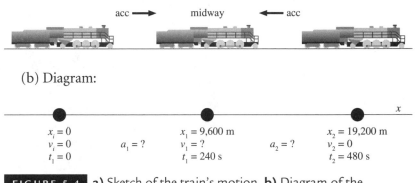

(b) Diagram:

FIGURE 5.4 **a)** Sketch of the train's motion. **b)** Diagram of the train's motion.

5. We must find a_1 and a_2. It will turn out that we must also find v_1 in order to determine the accelerations.

✔ **QUICK CHECK**

Can you prepare a strategy for finding a_1 and a_2? (Hint: Will anything we developed in Chapter 3 be of use?)

Answer: In Chapter 3, we found that $\Delta x = v_i t + \dfrac{1}{2} a_1 t^2$. We can use this equation to find a_1. However, we can't use it directly to find a_2, because we don't know v_1. But we can find v_1 in either of two ways: from $v_1 = v_i + a_1 t$ or from $v_1^2 - v_i^2 = 2a_1(x_1 - x_i)$. Then we can find a_2.

COMPLETED EXAMPLE

Find a_1, v_1, and a_2 from the information in our table and Figure 5.4 and from the equations in the previous paragraph.

Step 1: To find a_1, use $x_1 - x_i = v_i t + \frac{1}{2}a_1 t_1^2$, which becomes

$$9{,}600 \text{ m} - 0 = 0 + \frac{1}{2}a_1(240 \text{ s})^2.$$

Thus, $a_1 = \dfrac{2(9{,}600 \text{ m})}{(240 \text{ s})^2} = \dfrac{9{,}600}{(120)(240)}\dfrac{\text{m}}{\text{s}^2} = \dfrac{80 \text{ m}}{240 \text{ s}^2} = \dfrac{1 \text{ m}}{3 \text{ s}^2} = 0.333 \dfrac{\text{m}}{\text{s}^2}.$

This solution also illustrates that we don't always have to use a calculator, but instead can simplify fractions.

Step 2: To find v_1:

Method 1: $v_1 = v_i + a_1(t_1 - t_i) = v_i + a_1 t_1$.

$$v_1 = 0 + 0.333 \frac{\text{m}}{\text{s}^2}(240 \text{ s}) = 80 \frac{\text{m}}{\text{s}}.$$

Method 2: $v_1^2 - v_i^2 = 2a_1(x_1 - x_i)$, so

$$v_1^2 = 2\left(0.333 \frac{\text{m}}{\text{s}^2}\right)(9{,}600 \text{ m}) = 6{,}400 \frac{\text{m}^2}{\text{s}^2} \text{ and } v_1 = 80 \frac{\text{m}}{\text{s}}.$$

Step 3: To find a_2:

Method 1. (Not the easiest method. Can you think of an easier one?)
Use $x_2 - x_1 = v_1(t_2 - t_1) + \frac{1}{2}a_2(t_2 - t_1)^2.$

PRACTICE

Solve this equation for a_2. This requires a higher level of mental practice than the concrete operations where we just put in numbers right away.

Solution: Start with $x_2 - x_1 - v_1(t_2 - t_1) = \frac{1}{2}a_2(t_2 - t_1)^2$, so

$$a_2 = \frac{2[(x_2 - x_1) - v_1(t_2 - t_1)]}{a_2(t_2 - t_1)^2}.$$

Now we find that $a_2 = \dfrac{2\left[9{,}600 \text{ m} - \left(80 \dfrac{\text{m}}{\text{s}^2}\right)(240 \text{ s})\right]}{(240 \text{ s})^2} = -\dfrac{1 \text{ m}}{3 \text{ s}^2} = -0.333 \dfrac{\text{m}}{\text{s}^2}.$

Method 2: Use $v_2 = v_1 + a_2(t_2 - t_1)$. This is easier, but it's important to be well-acquainted with all possible ways of solving these problems.

✔ **QUICK CHECK**

Why is a_2 negative?

Answer: The negative acceleration is not caused by the train slowing down. Be careful of making that error. The acceleration is negative because we chose the positive direction of the x-axis, the coordinate axis, in the direction of the initial velocity in our diagram in Figure 4.2(b). If you go back and check the figure, you will see a small x at the right on the coordinate axis. The velocity and acceleration v_1 and a_1 are positive because the train moves to the right and the velocity, directed to the right, is increasing. The velocity and acceleration v_2 and a_2 are positive and negative, respectively, because the train keeps on moving to the right even though it is slowing down. Here the acceleration is directed opposite to the velocity and is therefore in the negative direction relative to the coordinate axis.

Other Forces

PROBLEMS IN ELECTROSTATICS

Let's look at a problem that involves two charged bodies.

WORKED EXAMPLE 5.4

Suppose that two tiny spheres made of an electrically conducting material are hanging by insulating threads. Both spheres are positively charged, the one on the left with a $+3.0\ \mu C$ charge and the one on the right with a $+4.0\ \mu C$ charge. At what angle θ do the two threads hang? Each sphere has a mass of 5.0 g.

Plan your strategy for solving this problem, then read on.

1. Draw a sketch of the charged spheres just described.

   Remember that charges of the same sign repel one another and charges of opposite signs attract:

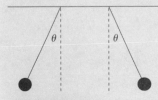

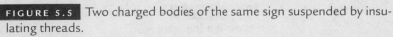

FIGURE 5.5 Two charged bodies of the same sign suspended by insulating threads.

2. Which laws do you need to know to make the sketches physically correct?

You need to ask why both angles are indicated by the same angle θ in Figure 5.5, even though the charges have different magnitudes, and ask what extra assumption we are making.

This is the same as asking how we know that the electrostatic force on the $+3.0\ \mu C$ charge has the same magnitude as the electrostatic force on the $+4.0\ \mu C$ charge.

(If the masses of the two spheres were not equal, they would hang at different angles.)

Because of Coulomb's law, the magnitudes of the forces that any two charges exert on one another are equal. This is also guaranteed by Newton's Third law.

If the electrostatic force on each sphere is directed away from the other charged sphere, each sphere will hang as shown. The vertical, gravitational, force is the same on each sphere. The electrostatic Coulomb force on each sphere has the same magnitude but opposite direction. A free body diagram will illustrate this better than words.

Now you are ready to draw a free-body diagram for either sphere, but let's concentrate on the one on the left.

TIME TO TRY

1. Draw a free body diagram for the sphere on the left in Figure 5.5. Then check the answer in Figure 5.6.

2. What is the sum of the three forces on the sphere in Figure 5.6?

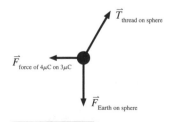

FIGURE 5.6   A free body diagram showing the forces on the sphere on the left in Figure 5.5.

Answer: We can show the forces another way. If we break the force that the thread exerts on the sphere down into components along the x- and y-axes, those components are equal and opposite to the other two forces on the sphere. This is shown in Figure 5.8.

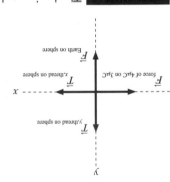

FIGURE 5.8 The horizontal and vertical components of the force that the thread exerts are shown as vector components. We then use the components for calculations.

When the sphere hangs at an angle, the horizontal component of the tension is equal and opposite to the electrostatic force. The vertical component of the tension is equal and opposite to the force of the Earth on the sphere. If we know the mass and the charges, we can calculate the angle of the insulating thread.

3. How do we use this information in calculations?

Answer: Because the sphere will take a position away from the other positive charge and then not move, its velocity is then not changing. If its velocity is not changing, its acceleration is zero. If its acceleration is zero, then there is no net external force on it. Therefore, the forces must add up to zero. Figure 5.7 shows that the sum of the forces is zero.

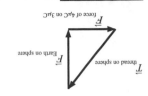

FIGURE 5.7 The three forces are added vectorially by placing the arrows head to tail. These forces do not sum to any fourth vector. Their sum is zero.

WORKED EXAMPLE 5.5

Complete the calculation:

If the mass of each sphere is 5.00 g, find the angle θ at which each thread hangs.

Answer:

We know the following:

$$m = 0.00500 \text{ kg} \qquad q_1 = 3.00 \ \mu C \qquad q_2 = 4.00 \ \mu C$$

$$k = 9.00 \times 10^9 \ \frac{\text{N} \cdot \text{m}^2}{\text{C}^2} \qquad g = 9.80 \ \frac{\text{m}}{\text{s}^2}$$

We also have the basic equations:

$$F_{3 \ \mu C \text{ on } 4 \ \mu C} = \frac{k(3 \ \mu C)(4 \ \mu C)}{r^2} = \frac{k(4 \ \mu C)(3 \ \mu C)}{r^2} = F_{4 \ \mu C \text{ on } 3 \ \mu C}, \text{ and}$$

$$F_{3 \mu C, g} = mg = F_{4 \mu C, g}.$$

The two equations relating the tension components to the physical forces are obtained by looking at Figure 5.8 and observing that the forces in the x-direction and the forces in the y-direction must separately sum to zero if the sphere is to stand still when at an angle. Thus,

$$T_x = F_{4 \ \mu C \text{ on } 3 \mu C}$$

$$T_y = F_{\text{Earth on sphere}}$$

Next we use trigonometry to show that $T_x = T \sin \theta$ and $T_y = T \cos \theta$, where θ is the angle between the tension T and the y-axis. (See Figure 5.5 where θ is shown.) Then,

$$T \sin \theta = \frac{kq_1q_2}{r^2} \qquad \qquad \text{Eqn. 5.1}$$

$$T \cos \theta = mg \qquad \qquad \text{Eqn. 5.2}$$

where the two charges are q_1 and q_2 and r is the distance from one charge to the other.

Now here's a trick we often use: Divide Equation 5.1 by Equation 5.2, left side by left side and right side by right side. You get

$$\frac{\sin \theta}{\cos \theta} = \tan \theta = \frac{kq_1q_2}{mgr^2}.$$

We can solve this for θ, because

$$\tan \theta = \frac{9.00 \times 10^9 \frac{N \cdot m^2}{C^2}(3.00 \times 10^{-6} \text{ C})(4.00 \times 10^{-6} \text{ C})}{(0.005 \text{ kg})\left(9.80 \frac{m}{s^2}\right)(1.00 \text{ m})^2} = 2.20.$$

Use your calculator to find the angle from $\tan^{-1} \theta$ to get the result:

$$\theta = 65.6°.$$

This problem shows how strong the electrostatic force is compared to the gravitational force. Two very small charges exert forces on one another that are a bit larger than the force exerted by the whole Earth on each sphere.

Estimates

Why take up estimates again? Because they are vitally important in many situations. For example: Can I afford to live off-campus? If I buy that dress, will I ever wear it again? Will these running shoes last long enough to justify their cost? Can I afford to pay for tuition and a car?

Engineers and scientists start with rough calculations before going to the expense of building models. Then they often build a model before designing a super-expensive chemical plant or refinery. For instance: Hydrogen is highly explosive—how thick of a steel panel must surround the engine in a hydrogen-fueled car in order to protect the occupants? Is it so massive that the car has too low an acceleration? How many acres of corn are needed to produce biofuel that would replace 50% of imported oil? How many windmills are needed to replace all other sources of electrical energy in the United States?

Let's try this last estimate.

WORKED EXAMPLE 5.6

Try this for yourself. Note that you can estimate the number of people in the country and how much electrical energy each uses. You may need to find a source of information about windmill energy generation on the Web. Also note that electrical power is supplied as watts, joules per second, where the joule is the unit of energy. You must multiply the power used by the time over which it is used to get the energy used. See what answer you get, and then read the following answer.

Answer: There are approximately 300,000,000 people in the United States. While there are many families, there are also many college-age students, divorced people, and elderly people who live alone. Let's estimate 150,000,000 households. Each of these, except for those abjectly poor, has a refrigerator, a TV, electronic devices, washing machines, etc. Even those living in apartments use washing machines and dryers, so we can include them in our estimate for everybody.

A possible estimate of power use is 2,000 W for 12 hours a day. That's 24 kWh of energy. To find the energy used in a year, we must multiply that estimate by 365 for the number of days in each year. More formally, we have

$$\frac{24 \text{ kWh}}{\text{family, day}} \cdot \frac{365 \text{ days}}{\text{year}} = \frac{8,760 \text{ kWh}}{\text{family, year}}.$$

This just says that each family uses 8,760 kWh in a 365-day year. Because this is an estimate, we have not used 365.25 days or any further such correction. For a rough calculation, we could have rounded the year to 400 days.

Now we multiply by the total number of households to find the energy used in the whole country. We multiply by 150,000,000 and find the energy used is $\frac{1.3 \times 10^{11} \text{ kWh}}{\text{family, year}}$.

However, we have neglected schools, street lighting, stores, theaters, and all other such energy users. Let's double the number. None of this could be paid for unless there were employment—and some factories, such as those that manufacture aluminum, use a lot of energy. So let's double the number again. We get

$$4 \times \left(1.3 \times 10^{11} \frac{\text{kWh}}{\text{y}} \right) = 5.2 \times 10^{12} \frac{\text{kWh}}{\text{y}}.$$

About 6 to 7×10^{12} kWh were used in 2006, so we know this number is in the ballpark.

If we assume a modern windmill can produce 1 MW (megawatt = 1 million watts) half the time, then in a year it can produce

$$1 \text{ MW} \times \frac{12 \text{ h}}{\text{day}} \times 365 \text{ days} = 4.4 \times 10^6 \text{ kWh}.$$

If we divide the total amount of energy used by the energy produced by each—a more technical way of saying it would be "per"—windmill, we find that

$$N = \frac{5.2 \times 10^{12} \frac{\text{kWh}}{\text{y}}}{4.4 \times 10^6 \frac{\text{kWh}}{\text{y}}} \approx 10^6.$$

Thus, one million windmills would be needed.

✔ **QUICK CHECK**

How many windmills is this for each state in the United States? Assume each state has the same number of windmills.

Answer: The number per state is $n_{state} = \frac{1 \times 10^6}{50} = 20{,}000$. That's not too unreasonable a number, and it should decrease as windmill technology improves.

Students often dislike estimates because there is no single clear formula to use to determine them. If you examine this illustrative estimate carefully, you will see that we are not doing anything different from what reporters do, and they are people who typically have studied a lot less math than physics students such as those who are using this book.

✔ **QUICK CHECK**

What questions did we answer? Look at the estimate and make a list of the questions that were asked and answered in each step.

Answer: Here is a simplified analysis: 1. How many households are there? 2. How much electrical energy was used by each household? This included the rate of use and the time period over which the power was used. Here energy was power x time. 3. What other uses were there (those not at home)? 4. How much energy did those other users consumer? 5. How much electrical energy could each windmill produce? 6. How many windmills were required? This was the ratio of total electrical energy to that produced by one windmill.

WORKED EXAMPLES 5.7

Here are some simple estimate problems. First list the questions you must answer. Then list your answers to them. Finally, complete the estimate. (Note: Remember that the U.S. population is around 300,000,000.)

1. How many fingers are there on people in the United States?

2. How many toes are there on people in the United States?

3. How many pizzas are eaten in the United States in a year?

4. How many classes do college students attend in the United States in a year?

Answers:

1. How many people? 300,000,000. We can ignore injuries (lost fingers) because the number is a small fraction of the total. How many fingers per person? Usually 10. Because $3 \times 10^8 \times 10 = 3 \times 10^9$, the number of fingers is 3 billion.

2. The answer is the same as that for (1).

3. Babies and very old people don't usually eat pizza, whereas students and young families typically eat a lot of it. Let's guess about 1 to 2 pizzas for each household each week. Stated more technically, 1 to 2 pizzas per household per week, but *per* simply means "for each." That way, 1.5×10^8 households times 52 weeks times 1 or 2 pizzas gives us 8×10^9 to 16×10^9 pizzas per year.

4. To make this estimate, you first have to estimate the number of U.S. college students. There are fewer older people than younger people in the United States. If we assume equal numbers of people of ages up to 60, and four years in college (both imperfect assumptions), then about $\frac{1}{15}$ of the population is college age. About half of this population attends college, so $\frac{1}{2} \cdot \frac{1}{15} \cdot (300{,}000{,}000) = 10{,}000{,}000$ students. An average of 5 courses meeting 3 times a week for 30 weeks gives 450 classes per student each year. Therefore, there are $450 \times 10^7 = 4.5 \times 10^9 \approx 5 \times 10^9$ or 5 billion student classes to be attended each year.

At 30 students per class, how many separate classes are there?

Can you estimate how many of these classes are actually attended? (Note: See Chapter 1. The students who cut lots of classes will also *repeat* lots of classes.)

MORE ON ESTIMATES

Other estimates, some of importance, might be as follows:

How many gallons of gasoline are used in the United States each year?

If people lived on bread alone, how many loaves of bread would have to be provided each year to feed everyone on the Earth (about 9 billion people)?

In a famous poem by Catullus, he asks his love to give him a thousand kisses and then a thousand more. How much time would be needed for a thousand times a thousand kisses?

How many water molecules are there in a human body, which is approximately 65% water.

In the book *Numeracy*, John Paulos estimates how many gallons of human blood there are in the world. How many vampires would that support for a year, if we assume that a vampire has the same need for caloric intake as a normal human being?

In short, estimates can be dead serious, as in estimates of food and fuel needs, or they can be about curiosities. They all come down to basic estimates or information about how many, how much, how long a time, what area or volume, and other basic quantities.

ESTIMATES AND CHECKING ANSWERS

TAKING A WRONG TURN Suppose you were taking a trip by car in 1980. Neither MapQuest nor GPS systems were available. You had to consult a map or get directions from another person, possibly a stranger. Even with MapQuest's help it's not always obvious which fork in a road is the continuation of the road and which is the wrong choice. It's still possible to make a mistake and hear that nagging voice that says something's wrong, whether it's inside your head or it comes from the

GPS system. In either case, we realize we have to turn back or find an alternate route.

The same sorts of mental skills are needed when an e-mail from Nigeria tells you to send $10,000 in order to release a $10 million reward. It's hard to believe, but even educated people fall for these scams. Would there be so much spam in e-mail otherwise? No one is giving away large amounts of money to strangers. And beautiful women from Russia are out to marry an unknown man only to acquire U.S. citizenship, and any possible divorce settlement.

How do you know when your solution to a physics problem has taken a wrong turn because you married yourself to a wrong assumption? What do you do when you don't get the award of a final answer that is reasonably easy to calculate? Or even if you do, how can you recognize an unreasonable answer?

WORKED EXAMPLES 5.8

The following items give a quick summary of a problem and a sample answer. Decide whether or not the answer is reasonable. Write down the criteria you use.

1. A plane accelerates down a 1,000 m-long runway and lifts off into the air at the end of the runway 10 s after it started from rest. Student A's solution has found the acceleration to be $2\,\frac{m}{s^2}$.

   This acceleration is about one-fifth of g, the acceleration gravity produces. That seems low. We know that a plane needs a large acceleration in order to lift off before running out of runway. A quick estimate of $\frac{1}{2}at^2$, with $a = 2\,\frac{m}{s^2}$ and $t = 10$ s, gives us a distance of 100 m, not 1,000 m. This shows that the correct answer must be $20\,\frac{m}{s^2}$.

2. A 1,500 kg car has locked bumpers with a 2,000 kg car. The 2,000 kg car's bumper is on top of the 1,500 kg car's bumper. Student B's calculation finds that a 20,000 N force (approximately 4,400 pounds) is needed to lift the 2,000 kg car's bumper off the 1,500 kg car's bumper.

The force is large, but it might be reasonable. However, you only need to lift the back of the car. The engine is probably in the front, since these are old cars that have bumpers. The weight of the heavier car, the force the Earth exerts on it, is $mg = 19,600$ N. We'd expect that we need to support only half that weight, so 10,000 N should do it. To the extent that the ground supports the front half of the car and the engine, a smaller force will actually do it. Because a mass of 1,000 kg is equivalent to a weight of 2,200 pounds, about one ton of force should do the trick.

3. A salesperson who knows some physics tells you that a 12 V, 100 A-hour battery stores 4,320,000 J of energy. (Remember that 1 volt times 1 ampere = 1 joule/second.)

   This seems large, but a joule is a small amount of energy. If you lift 250 g 1 m, you've done less than 0.250 J of work on the ball. We need to check the math: $12 \text{ V} \times 100 \text{ A} \times 3,600 \text{ s} = 1,200 \frac{\text{J}}{\text{s}} \times 3,600 \text{ s} = 4,320,000$ J. You may know that 1 volt $\times$ 1 ampere $= 1$ watt and 1 watt $= 1 \dfrac{\text{joule}}{\text{second}}$. The basic principle here is that power—energy per unit of time—multiplied by the time interval, equals energy. It takes a lot of energy to start a car. Have you ever seen an old movie where the chauffeur had to crank the engine by hand to start the car?

4. A real image is formed on a screen by the lens in a slide projector. One of the people in your study group says that if you cover half the lens you will see the whole image. (Hint: Light rays from every point on the slide hit every point of the lens.)

   This may seem amazing, but consider this: The light source is behind the slide. Therefore, light rays come out of every point of the slide and move off in every direction from every point of the slide. Light rays from every point of the slide reach every point of the lens. The lens brings all the light rays from one point on the slide together at one point of the image. All that changes when we cover half the lens is the intensity of the image because half of the rays do not make it to the screen. The statement is correct.

5. A 4,000 kg truck traveling at 30 $\frac{m}{s}$ comes to a screeching halt and narrowly misses hitting a car driven by an 80-year-old woman who just ignored a red light. An observer who knows some physics states that the truck's tires now contain 1,800,000 J of thermal energy.

It is true that $\frac{1}{2}m_{truck}v_{truck}^2 = \frac{1}{2}(4{,}000\text{ kg})\left(30\ \frac{m}{s}\right)^2 = 1.8 \times 10^6$ J of kinetic energy has ended up as 1.8×10^6 J of internal thermal energy. However, this is a result of a frictional interaction between the tires and the road. The internal thermal energy is divided between the tires and the road, but we don't know what fraction of the total thermal energy ended up in the tires and what fraction ended up in the road. We do know it did not all end up in the tires. There also is a considerable amount of thermal energy in the brakes and wheels.

TIME TO TRY

True or False? Why?

1. A salesperson in Europe tells you that 2.2 pounds is the same as 1.0 kg.   T F

2. If you pitch a ball over the edge of a cliff, you can find it at the base of the cliff.   T F

3. If a body does not move when you bring an electrostatically charged object near it, that body is uncharged.   T F

4. Some atoms can be seen with the naked eye.   T F

5. You can never step twice in the same river.   T F

Answers: 1. F. The 1.0 kg mass weighs 9.8 Newtons (N) or 2.2 pounds at sea level; the kilogram is a unit of mass. The pound is a unit of force, like the Newton. However, we sometimes speak of a pound of "mass," and we mean that mass which weighs one pound. 2. F. The ball starts to be accelerated downward by gravity as soon as it leaves the hand but it also keeps the horizontal velocity it had when it left the hand because there is no force in the horizontal direction. (We are ignoring air resistance.) It continues to accelerate downward, therefore increasing its vertical velocity downward, while maintaining its horizontal velocity

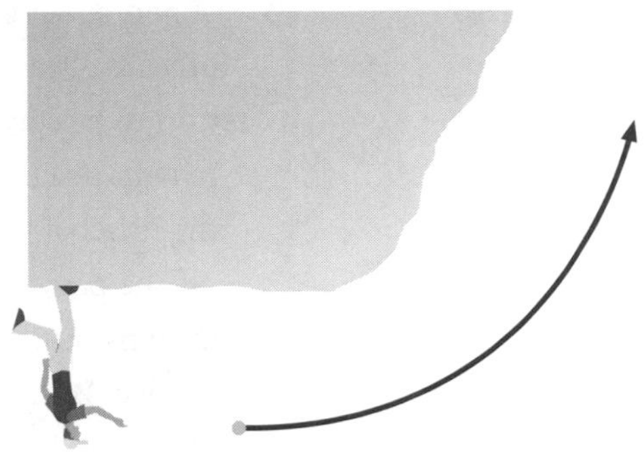

FIGURE 5.9   Path of a ball thrown in a horizontal direction near the edge of a cliff.

after passing the edge of the cliff. It moves faster and faster vertically downward while also moving horizontally at the same time. The net velocity is the vector sum of the horizontal velocity and vertical velocity at any particular time. Because the horizontal velocity never becomes zero when we neglect air resistance, the ball cannot be moving straight downward at any time. Therefore, its velocity is not perpendicular to the ground when it hits the ground. The greater the horizontal velocity when it leaves the hand, the farther from the cliff the ball falls. See Figure 5. 9. 3. F. The body may just be too heavy to be budged by a small electro-static force, because the force of friction between the body and what it is resting on matches the electrostatic force. Then the net force is zero and the body does not move. For example, a lead brick won't be moved by the charge on a piece of Scotch® tape. 4. F. Atoms are too small to be seen by the naked eye. For exam-ple, there can be about 10^8 water molecules—each of which contains three atoms—along an inch-long line. 5. T and F. You don't encounter the same water molecules unless some of them evaporated and returned to the river as rain; but if the flow maintains the same pattern—described by streamlines—then the aver-age positions, velocities, and accelerations of the water molecules you encounter the second time are the same as those of the water molecules you encountered the first time. This example shows how careful we have to be about what our words themselves mean.

Question 1 reflects a widespread confusion about mass versus weight. People in Europe speak of a kilogram as a weight when they mean that a kilogram would weigh 9.8 N. This can be confusing when solving physics problems, so you should distinguish clearly between masses and weights, since weights represent the net force that the Earth exerts on an object as measured by the force a scale must exert on it to keep it from falling through the scale. Mass is a measure of the amount of material that a substance or object contains.

Units and Dimensions: Another Way of Checking Answers

When solving problems for specific numerical answers, solutions in physics always have units attached: $m, \frac{m}{s}, \frac{m}{s^2}, N, J, C$, etc. For an equation to be correct, every term must have the same units. Otherwise we may have a length on one side of an equation and a length squared on the other side.

The basic types of physical quantities in any term or equation are its dimensions. The dimensions never change, although the units may change. Length is a dimension that can be measured in meters, or yards, or miles. Whichever unit we use, the dimension stays the same. Therefore, the units can be used to check for dimensional correctness. (Of course, if you use meters in one term and yards in another, your final answer will not be numerically correct. Because one team used English units and another team used the metric system, a Mars lander crashed.)

✔ QUICK CHECK

The following equations contain symbols or numbers with units, all of them used earlier in this book. Determine whether or not they are dimensionally correct. Then check again to be sure consistent units were used in each term. For help, check Table 5.1.

1. $5.0 \frac{m}{s} = 2.0 \frac{m}{s} + \left(1.5 \frac{m}{s^2}\right)(2.0 \text{ s}).$

2. $\left(8.0 \frac{m}{s}\right)^2 - \left(6.0 \frac{m}{s}\right) = 2\left(9.8 \frac{m}{s}\right)(1.43 \text{ m}).$

3. $F\Delta x = mv_f - mv_i.$

4. $81 \text{ N} = \left(9.0 \times 10^9 \frac{N \cdot m^2}{C^2}\right)\left(\frac{9.0 \ \mu C \times 9.0 \text{ mC}}{3.0 \text{ m}}\right).$

5. $\frac{1}{2}mv_i^2 + mgy_i + F^{ext}\Delta y = \frac{1}{2}mv_f^2 + mgy_f + \Delta E^{ext.thermal}.$

6. $-150 \text{ m} = \left(5.0 \frac{m}{s}\right)(10 \text{ s}) - \frac{1}{2}\left(20 \frac{cm}{s^2}\right)(10 \text{ s})^2.$

TABLE 5.1 Dimensions and units of some physical quantities.

Quantity	Name	Dimension	Unit
x	position	length	m
v	speed	length/time	$\dfrac{m}{s}$
a	acceleration	length/time^2	$\dfrac{m}{s^2}$
F	force	mass $\times$ distance/t^2	$kg \cdot \dfrac{m}{s^2}$
mass	mass	mass	kg
K	kinetic energy	$\dfrac{mass \times distance^2}{time^2}$	J
p	momentum	mass $\times$ distance/time	$kg \cdot \dfrac{m}{s}$
Ug	potential energy	$\dfrac{mass \times distance^2}{time^2}$	J
q	charge	charge	C
T	temperature	temperature	K
t	time	time	s

Answers: 1. Correct in dimensions, units, and numbers. 2. Incorrect in dimensions, units, and numbers because the person forgot to square the second term. 3. Incorrect. The left-hand side should read $F\Delta t$. 4. Incorrect, because the person forgot to square the denominator in the last term in parentheses. 5. Correct. 6. Incorrect, because centimeters and meters were mixed in the same equation.

Always make sure that the dimensions match in all terms in each equation, and that you use appropriate units. ■

Answering Conceptual Multiple-Choice Questions

Physics teachers use conceptual multiple-choice problems to check students' understanding of physics systems and models; some use it because it takes less time than it takes to show understanding by solving a problem.

Unless you understand the underlying physics, memorization of methods for solving individual problems and of equations will fail to help you when a new variation appears on an exam. ■

We discussed general approaches to multiple-choice questions in Chapter 1. Here we'll look at how to approach conceptual multiple-choice questions so that you can avoid answering on the basis of preconceptions.

WORKED EXAMPLES 5.9

Here are six multiple-choice questions. Circle the correct answer(s) in each one.

1. Which, if any, of the following relations between velocity and acceleration are not possible over any time period?

   a. The velocity is constant and the acceleration is positive.

   b. The velocity is positive and the acceleration is positive.

   c. The velocity is positive and the acceleration is negative.

   d. The velocity is negative and the acceleration is positive.

   e. The velocity is negative and the acceleration is negative.

   f. The velocity is constant and the acceleration is negative.

First think about the following questions. If you do not instinctively agree with the answers that immediately follow, you need to think about why the answers are correct.

i. What determines whether any physical quantity is positive or negative?

   The coordinate axis you chose determines which direction is positive and which is negative. You are free to reverse the direction of the coordinate axis. That would change the signs of the physical quantities, but would not change what is going on at all. Always remember that the math is what we add in order to represent the world by numbers.

ii. What is happening when the velocity is in the same direction as the acceleration?

If the acceleration is in the same direction as the velocity, the velocity is increasing in magnitude.

iii. What is happening when the velocity is in the direction opposite to the acceleration?

If the acceleration is opposite in direction to the velocity, the velocity is decreasing in magnitude.

Now check your answers to (1) again, and revise them if necessary.

Answer:

1. Only (a) and (f) are not possible, because the velocity must change if the acceleration is not zero. Remember that acceleration is defined as the time rate of change of velocity.

This question tested whether or not you understand the distinction between velocity and acceleration, and, just as important, whether or not you understand what it means to say that something is positive or negative. Note also that a constant velocity must be positive or negative, but a positive or negative velocity does not have to be constant. Thus, this question also tested your ability to read closely and make fine distinctions.

2. You toss a ball straight up and catch it as it returns to your hand. A ball stops when you catch it in your hand because

a. your hand is there: You exert no force on the ball.

b. your hand exerts a frictional force on the ball, perpendicular to the ball's velocity.

c. your hand exerts a force on the ball in the direction of its velocity.

d. your hand exerts a force on the ball in the direction opposite to its velocity.

e. your hand exerts a force equal to its velocity on the ball.

Consider the following questions and answers:

i. What is the system here?

The system is the ball.

ii. What are the forces on that system?

The forces on the ball are the upward force exerted by the hand and the downward force exerted by the Earth. Note that velocity is not the same as force, so answer (e) is an attempt to mislead you. Newton's Second law says that acceleration is proportional to *change* in velocity. Once again we are ignoring the effect of air resistance.

Answer: The correct answer is (d). To slow the ball down, the acceleration must be opposite to its velocity. Therefore, if the ball is moving downward, the acceleration must be directed upward. Your hand exerts the force that produces the acceleration upward. That force must be upward, directed opposite to the direction of the ball's velocity.

3. You start with two identical beakers. Beaker A contains 10 g of water at 20°C; beaker B contains 1,000 g of water at 20°C. You center each beaker on a hot plate, and heat each beaker until the water in it starts boiling. When we compare the beakers' states at the times when the water in them is boiling, we can then conclude that

a. beakers A and B are at the same temperature and contain the same quantity of thermal energy.

b. beaker A is at the same temperature as beaker B but contains a greater amount of thermal energy.

c. beaker B is at the same temperature as beaker A but contains a greater amount of thermal energy.

d. beaker A is at a higher temperature but beaker B contains more thermal energy.

e. beaker B is at a higher temperature but beaker A contains more thermal energy.

Consider the following questions and answers:

i. How do you measure the temperature of a liquid?

    You would use a thermometer.

ii. Would you need to use different instruments to measure the temperature of the two samples?

    You could use the same thermometer, especially because it would take the larger quantity of liquid a longer time to reach the boiling point.

iii. How would you measure the thermal energy content of a liquid, or any other substance?

    Suppose you spilled the boiling liquid on yourself. Which would produce a worse and larger burn: 10 g, a fraction of an ounce, or 1,000 g, about the same as a quart? The larger quantity of liquid would transfer more thermal energy to your skin. In principal, we can measure thermal energy by seeing the temperature change that it produces in a given amount of a test substance under ideal conditions.

Answer: Our answers to the extra questions tell us that (c) is the correct answer. Note how the answer to question (iii) can lead you to the correct answer in spite of a possible temptation to choose answer (a).

The following two questions test different aspects of the same situation. Answers for both follow question 5:

4. Four small charged spheres, A, B, C, and D, are glued to an insulating surface so that they are at the corners of a square (Figure 5.10). Each sphere has a charge of the same magnitude, but two are positively charged and two are negatively charged. A fifth charge of equal magnitude is placed at P, the center of the square. Each of the other charges exerts a force of magnitude *F* on it. The net force on P is

   a. 0.

   b. *F*.

c. $\sqrt{2}F$.

d. 2*F*.

e. 4*F*.

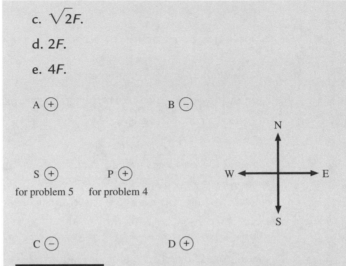

FIGURE 5.10   Charge P (question 4) or charge S (question 5) in the presence of four charges at the corners of a square.

5. Suppose instead you placed the fifth charge at point S instead of at point P. The direction of the force on the charge at S is

a. east.

b. north.

c. west.

d. south

e. northeast.

Consider the following questions and answers:

i. How do the magnitudes of the forces that A, B, C, and D exert on P compare to one another?

They are all equal in magnitude because the charges are equal in magnitude and the distances between the other charges and P are equal in magnitude.

ii. What are the directions of the forces that A, B, C, and D exert on P?

A and D exert forces that are opposite in direction on P. B and C exert forces that are opposite in direction on P.

iii. How do the magnitudes of the forces that A, B, C, and D exert on S compare to one another?

A and C exert forces of equal magnitude on S. B and D exert forces of equal magnitude on S, but these forces are smaller than those exerted by A and C.

iv. What are the directions of the forces that A, B, C, and D exert on S?

A and C exert forces that are directed down to the south on S. B exerts a force to the northeast on S and D exerts a force to the northwest on S.

Answers:

4. The forces are equal in magnitude and paired in opposite directions. The sum of all the forces is zero, so the answer is (a).

5. A and C produce forces to the south. The west component of the force from D is equal and opposite to the east component of the force from B. Those components cancel. That leaves the components directed north of the forces from B and D. Because the forces from B and D are smaller than the forces from A and C in the first place, the north components added together are less than the two south forces from A and C. Therefore, the net force is to the south. The answer is (d).

When solving conceptual multiple-choice problems, ask yourself as many questions as you can think of about the interactions, directions, and signs of forces, velocities, accelerations, displacements, charges, electric fields, and any other applicable concepts. ■

Final Stretch!

Now that you have finished reading this chapter it is time to stretch your brain and check how much you have learned.

WHAT DID YOU LEARN?

- How to use a strategy to solve a problem. This includes

    - how to select a system,

    - how to use different representations of the physical situation, and

    - how to select the appropriate model.

- How to use estimates to help you look for a strategy and to check your results

- Use of conservation laws for energy and momentum

- How to approach conceptual multiple-choice questions

WEB RESOURCES

For additional help, enter any of the topics listed in "What Did You Learn?" or boldface section titles in Google or another search engine. Again, Wikipedia will give you a very high-level overview, so you should look for sites at an appropriate level.

You will be able to find appropriate entries under "work-energy bar charts," "dimensions and units," "strategies; solving physics problems," and "estimates," but the author has only been able to find research articles when trying to search for "aids in defining systems when problem-solving." Because defining a system is an art as well as a skill, you will need to pay careful attention to how your teachers do that in class.

Index